# Fur and Freedom:
## In Defence of the Fur Trade

**Richard North**

With a Foreword by Professor Roger Scruton

Published by the IEA Environment Unit, 2000

First published in March 2000 by
The Environment Unit
The Institute of Economic Affairs
2 Lord North Street
Westminster
London SW1P 3LB

IEA Studies on the Environment No. 16
ISBN 0-255 36486-5

Printed in Great Britain by Hartington Fine Arts Limited, Lancing, West
Sussex

# Contents

4

# Preface

Is it morally acceptable to wear fur, and to farm, trap or sell mink and fox? Groups such as People for the Ethical Treatment of Animals (PETA) and Greenpeace say not. They have campaigned to make us abhor the very idea of fur. Yet what is the foundation of this moral imperative that they try to foist upon us? That to use animals in this way is wrong? But why might that be? The answer to these questions, as Richard North shows in this fascinating monograph, is not as obvious as many campaigners make out.

The views expressed in this monograph are those of the author and not of the IEA (which has no corporate view), its Directors, Advisors, or Trustees.

Julian Morris

Director, Environment Unit

January 2000

# Foreword

Nobody has succeeded in explaining why it is wrong to farm animals for their fur, but acceptable to farm them for their meat, or why the wearing of fur-coats is so heinous compared with the wearing of leather shoes. For some years, nevertheless, groups which claim to speak for 'animal rights' have been campaigning for a ban, and it is presumably not insignificant that one such group - the Political Animal Lobby - made a large donation to the Labour Party before the last election. In any case, the government has announced, through the recent Queen's Speech, that it intends to ban fur-farming in this country. It is wrong to take cash for questions, but OK to take cash for policies.

The muddle in which we find ourselves as a result of the movement for 'animal rights' is well illustrated by the RSPCA, one of the campaigning groups which is opposed to fur-farming. A circular recently came round from that organisation telling all members to write to the Prime Minister supporting his policy to ban hunting with dogs. I was mildly astonished to discover that the animal illustrated as the heart-stopping beneficiary of this humane initiative was not a bright little fox-cub, but a mink, its lethal incisors bared, and its close-set evil eyes clearly focused on some enemy - presumably one of those sanctimonious RSPCA inspectors who make even gentle old ladies bare their fangs. The circular told us that the use of dogs to hunt mink is unacceptable, and recommended instead that the animals be caught in traps, and subsequently dispatched (presumably after a day or so of leisurely retirement behind bars) by a humane killer.

At the same time, the RSPCA's ostensible reason for opposing the fur trade is that it is intolerable to mink to be trapped behind bars. Putting the two campaigns together one might conclude that the RSPCA - or at least its campaigning arm - does not in fact care about mink at all. It has merely conceived a hatred, first for those who wear fur, secondly for those who follow hounds (mink-hounds included). On the mistaken view that fur-wearers and hunt followers are both toffs, and that toffs ought to be persecuted, you might just begin to see sense in this combination of attitudes. But it is surely not the basis for wise or humane legislation.

As Richard North demonstrates, the arguments against the fur trade are entirely spurious, and would, if valid, rule out the trades in beef, pork, poultry, eggs and leather, not to speak of cat-gut and neat's foot oil. The decision that a trade should be criminalised, without any proof of its immorality or any suggestion that it is socially divisive or environmentally destructive, and only because a pressure group has said so, is a novel departure in English government. That the decision should come at a time when Parliament has become ostentatiously permissive in all matters pertaining to traditional morality, suggests that we are passing through a period of unusual hypocrisy, in which morality has become a matter of fashionable posturing rather than a submission to conscience.

All who are concerned about the interface between morality and politics should read this pamphlet, which explores the way in which humans feed their dislike of other humans by sentimentalizing other species. It reminds us that we should be thankful that animals do not have rights; for this means that some of the living beings we encounter are not self-righteous prigs.

Roger Scruton

Malmesbury, January 2000

# Acknowledgements

During the past year I have been funded by the British Fur Trade Association (BFTA) to pursue an information project. The funding equated to about three months' working time. The idea originated with me and the agenda was determined far more by me than by the trade. I am grateful to the association for the open-minded attitude its members brought to a project whose main characteristic was that I made up my own mind what I thought and said.

This pamphlet is based on the information I gathered when carrying out the BFTA project. This past year or so I have worked quite closely on various projects with Roger Bate and Julian Morris of the IEA and feel great admiration for the dynamism, rigour and enterprise they bring to promoting serious, often counter-intuitive, thinking about 'green' issues, which are so often riddled with political correctness and humbug.

Many academics and others have been generous with their time. I hope I have understood and transmitted their insights and evidence.

# The Author

From 1990 to 1992, Richard North was Environment Columnist for the *Sunday Times*. Prior to that, from 1986 to 1990, he was Environment Correspondent for the *Independent*.

He is the author of *Life on a Modern Planet: A Manifesto for Progress* (Manchester University Press, 1995 and St Martin's Press, New York, 1995); *Fools For God* (Collins, 1987); *Schools for Tomorrow* (Green Books, 1987) *Working the Land* (with Charlie Pye-Smith, 1985); *The Real Cost* (Chatto and Windus, 1984); *Wild Britain* (Century, 1983); and *The Animals Report* (Penguin, 1982).

Recent pamphlets by Richard North include: *Hereditary Peers: The case as yet unheard* (Social Affairs Unit, 1999); and *The Hunt At Bay* (Wildlife Network, 1999).

# Introduction

1999 was a surprisingly good year for the British fur trade, and it ended a surprisingly good decade for this most disparaged of businesses.

It is true that some of the most obvious signs were and remain the reverse of cheerful. In November, the monarch, wearing a stunning designer fur coat, arrived in Parliament to deliver the Queen's speech in which she announced her Government is determination to introduce legislation banning fur farming. If enacted, the bill will deliver a New Labour manifesto commitment which had earlier in the year had backbench championing. In January 1999, Maria Eagle, the Labour MP, introduced her private member's bill which sought to ban the farming of fur in Great Britain.[1] Its principal grounds were that the trade was cruel and supplied a luxury trade[2]. It was talked out, and in effect died,

---

[1] The BFTA notes: It seems to have been the RSPCA which initiated the Bill when it wrote to MPs in October 1998 urging a Private Members Bill on fur farming. The report said that is was opposed to 'farming and trapping of (wild) animals for their fur'. In its report, the RSPCA offered the services of its Parliamentary Department to MPs. It said that the RSPCA has a large national press office, as well as regional press officers, who would ensure that 'your message is effectively transmitted to the public...(RSPCA) has enormous experience in synchronising advertising campaigns, prompting letter writing campaigns and (will) ensure that every aspect of your campaign is co-ordinated.'

[2] The Eagle Bill proposed: complete extinction of fur farms in the UK; power to compensate farmers, and making it a criminal offence to farm animals primarily for the commercial value of their fur. Maria Eagle's Press Release of 12 January 1999, headlined 'Maria Eagle goes for ban on Fur Trade', said she had decided to support the RSPCA and introduced the fur farm ban proposal because: fur farming is morally wrong because wild animals are 'farmed' and slaughtered for their fur; such practice is cruel and unnecessary; people have a repugnance at wearing fur; the fur trade has declined.

in July 1999, but its general principles have now been both adopted and developed.

Extraordinarily, Elliot Morley, the Countryside Minister, now uses the grounds of 'public morality' to defend the proposed ban. This language is new, and seems necessary mostly because there are few serious justifications for picking out fur farming as particularly bad except perhaps that large numbers of people profess themselves opposed to it. In other words, public 'morality' is now synonymous with public 'opinion'. Some of the obvious differences between the two are considered in Chapter 1. Anyway, ministers have elevated public opinion, however ill-informed, inflamed by media outpourings or transient, into what passes in a febrile age for ethical principle.

On the face of it, the prospect of a ban is bad news for the trade and good news for animals. The reality, however, is rather more complex. Indeed it can be plausibly argued that such a ban would be bad news for freedom, for good sense, and for fair play.

Indeed, very interesting aspects of the way modern societies work and think are on display as we watch events surrounding the fur trade. Such study is a wonderful opportunity to watch double-think, moral triviality, grandstanding and humbug at work on issues ranging from animal welfare through to thinking about the rich.

Maria Eagle's bill produced one major effect she may not have desired: a second sustained media discussion, which allowed the possibility that a ban of fur farming might be an oppressive use of the law (the first followed the release of mink from farms in August and September 1998, see below pp.37).

There are of course profound animal welfare issues in the use of fur, as there are in any other animal use. Few consumers of bacon sandwiches would consider their activity to be as morally problematic as wearing fur, and yet there are close parallels between them. A discussion of these issues will make up the second, animal welfare, part of what follows, as Chapter 2.

But the monograph begins with a consideration of the human side of the issue, in Chapter 1. The fur trade has long been subject to pressure from its opponents, who protest in various ways. Some assert, and respect, the right to protest in a more or less dignified and very public way. Some protesters noisily harangue the customers and staff of fur shops, whilst others go so far as to harass them. Others take the battle to the homes of anyone associated with the fur trade, and there the harassment takes on a new seriousness.

Much of this sort of protest looks like the entirely laudable if uncomfortable process of a vigorous democracy. Some of it is exactly that, and attracts a good deal of tacit public support. However, much of it is not. Unfortunately, the media rarely questions the motives or justifications given by anti-fur campaigners. As with so much agitation from environmentalists, animal rights activists and the like, lazy or inept journalists simply regurgitate press releases without a thought for the veracity of the claims made therein. Here, the issue is considered in a rather more sceptical way than is common.

Some protesters undertake direct action against fur farms, most famously in the summer of 1998 when they released mink into the wild. Because the releases brought about the first positive press coverage the fur trade had received for years, these issues are considered in Chapter 1 as the discussion is broadened to cover the media.

Chapter 1 also contains an analysis of the remarkable revival of the fortunes of the fur trade in recent years. Long castigated as a 'dying trade' by its enemies, it is actually flourishing (Table 1). It is clearly a 'luxury' trade, and as such is a bell-weather of the world's economy, and especially of the emerging economies, which provide large quantities of *nouveaux riches* seeking extravagant expression of their new found wealth. The trade's opponents seem to dislike it precisely because it thrives when the rich thrive, and they suppose that it only satisfies desires which only the rich can indulge. This latter prejudice is called into question and the merits of extravagance for its own sake contemplated.

## Table 1: World Mink Production 1980 - 1999[3]

| Year | Million Pelts | Comments |
|------|---------------|----------|
| 80 | 22 | |
| 81 | 23.3 | |
| 82 | 26.2 | |
| 83 | 27.9 | |
| 84 | 29.9 | |
| 85 | 32.6 | High |
| 86 | 33.8 | |
| 87 | 35.7 | Very high - all time peak |
| 88 | 41.7 | Price weakening |
| 89 | 38.5 | |
| 90 | 27.1 | |
| 91 | 26.1 | |
| 92 | 26.4 | Low |
| 93 | 20.4 | All time low |

[3]Figures are based on fur auction house returns. Some observations: In 1997 Danish mink production was about 45 per cent of total and four Times greater than its next competitor, the USA. In 1988, Scandinavian production was 19.5m (of which Denmark was 12.7m);USA 4.5m; Russia, 5m; Canada 1.3m; China, 5m; Holland 1.8m. In 1997, Scandinavian production was 14.8m (of which Denmark was 10.8m); USA 2.7m; Russia, 2m; Canada less than 1m; China less than 1m; Holland 0.8. England 100k, Ireland 160k, France 100k.

| 94 | 22.6 | |
|----|------|---|
| 95 | 25.7 | |
| 96 | 24.6 | Very high, Russia and China boom |
| 97 | 26.3 | |
| 98 | - | Weakened on Russia's economic chaos |
| 99 | - | Recovering |

Public attitudes are not quite what the protesters might hope, and even the media are getting around to producing better coverage of the fur trade. But even if it cannot hope that protest will go away or even much diminish, the fur trade is within its rights to hope that it will be offered a decent level of protection from the hard core activists, both by the police and in the courts. However, this area is full of dilemmas. Since the courts and police operate only under licence from Parliament, it is necessary to consider, in Chapter 3, how governments and the authorities respond to these issues, and how they ought to. What is the politicians' obligation to the protesters, customers and traders, and the animals, we will by then have discussed in some detail.

# 1. The Fur Trade: Cruel and Unnecessary?

Anyone associated with the fur trade knows that they are in a business which it is hardly polite to mention. The response of the majority of people on meeting a furrier is often a sort of shock that they have actually come across such a pariah. Many people are used to hearing or even mouthing opposition to the trade, and to hearing or mouthing vague support for all the famous and attractive people who declare themselves its enemies. Actually to meet the object of all this dislike is a little surprising.

But something else happens too. People go on to say they do not approve of violent protest, and - almost by the way - women often add what fun it was when one could wear one's furs, and are such times really dead and gone?

It is, by the way, not merely the elderly or rich who now remember wearing fur: there is a generation of middle aged women of all sorts who wore fur in the 60s and 70s, often buying it in junk or charity shops, or inheriting from grandmothers and mothers.

Still, it is often a surprise for people to meet someone working in or supporting the trade. It is as though one had said one was an undertaker, or a slaughterhouse worker, even a paedophile. It would be better to say that one was a burglar than to admit to being a furrier. Now obviously these are all different cases. An undertaker gives people the creeps, though we know the job is respectable. A slaughterhouse worker is somehow more shocking, as though only a callous person could do such work, though such workers are thought to be somehow blamelessly manual. A paedophile would be disdained as a pervert as well as a criminal, but at least has the merit of being ill. A burglar might even be thought to have a certain glamour: think how celebrities courted the gang bosses of the Sixties.

So how to get the heart of the special dislike of the fur trade? The best image is that of Cruella De Vil, the witch-like bitch queen in Walt Disney's 101 Dalmations. She has a monstrous love of glamour, and a mighty disdain for the suffering she causes as she achieves it. She is, after all, the Devil. She has the same element of the joyously diabolical as we find in the Absolutely Fabulous females: we know they are atrocious, but we hope they win over more boringly scrupulous types. Cruella has the best lines in the movie, too.

There is assumed to be an element of torture in the fur trade, Cruella's own, of course, which is not present in most other uses of animals. The same sort of hatred does attach, however, to vivisectionists, as people who use live animals in any way in experiments are still called, though few actually cut into their animals, or indeed inflict serious pain. They are somehow assumed to be heartless people in pursuit of heartless science, or validation - more trivially - of unnecessary cosmetics. Hollywood has its own demonology for such people (especially in kids-or-dogs-films, such as Beethoven and the Babe movies).

But the Cruella image might seem well applied to furriers because their trade is perceived to deal to an extraordinary degree in waste and luxury. Maria Eagle caught this sense exactly in her bill which sought to ban fur farming. It emphasised the cruelty of the production methods on the one hand, but it pointedly juxtaposed the extravagance of the final product on the other. It aimed, she told the House of Commons on the first day of debate on her Fur Farming (Prohibition) Bill to outlaw 'the cruel exploitation of essentially wild animals for what is an inessential luxury item.' (*The Times*, 1999b). This interlocking of elements was felt to be a killer blow: one might justify suffering which was caused by necessity and one might justify luxury which did not involve suffering. But causing suffering just for luxury was clearly doubly wrong. It was also a situation unique to the fur trade, and expressed the uniqueness of the wrong done by the trade.

The same simplicity could not be applied, for instance, to vivisection, which comes bundled with different degrees of usefulness, and indeed is now more or less outlawed for cosmetic purposes.

## Unpicking the Arguments

Now to unpick some of this. It is clearly the case that people are within their rights to believe that man's use of animals is not justified by any human purpose. The animal rights case, in most of its forms, depends crucially on reminding ourselves that in the wild, 'nature' has ordained what happens to animals, and however awful that may be, at least humans may say that it is no fault of theirs. Provided humans stand back from nature, none of the suffering of animals is a moral charge on people.

The more 'hard-line' an animal rights case is being made, the less the usefulness or extravagance of the outcome matters. A hard-line animal rights view no more attacks useful animal experimentation than trivial experimentation. The human outcome is not in issue: the animal impact is. From a strict animal rightist point of view, it should make no difference the purpose for which an animal died. Such a view dislikes the way high human purposes might be put into the balance against animal suffering. The animal's supposed right is to non-interference, not merely to have its interests weighed in the balance.

Most of the serious (and dangerous) protesters against the fur trade are vegan. That is: they believe no animal consumption by humans can be justified. The 'hard' vegan case does not discriminate between food for the hungry, say, or pigs killed for bacon sandwiches for the overweight. It just says man should not kill animals for food.

There is of course ordinary merit in views much less extreme than this. Many of us distinguish between the human benefit derived from different forms of animal suffering. If there came to be a choice between using animals in research and using them in coats, most of us would prefer to defend the former, even if the former caused more suffering.

Whether one is against vivisection or merely against eating animals, such positions are capable of logical defence, have emotional appeal and may even be sensible.

17

The right to hold this sort of opinion is not in question. Arguably, it is the most noble sort of opinion about animals a person can hold. But many arguments which sought to defend the interests of animals would not by themselves stigmatise the fur-trade any more than they stigmatised the keeping of pigs for bacon, of cows for milk, the hunting of fox for fun and conservation, or the hunting of deer, or any other use.

The harder the animal rights case a person puts, the less can that person sensibly stigmatise the fur trade for the luxury of the outcome. Most animal production is undertaken for human pleasure, not human need. It makes no more sense to shout at a furrier than to shout at a butcher. It is just easier, and easier to get away with it in a society which does not care to think about such things. This is not the place to argue the legitimacy of man's treatment of animals.[4] It is only necessary here to argue that the fur trade has no harder a case to argue than any other trade using animal products.

Maria Eagle's bill argued that in the special case of fur, the suffering of animals is compounded by the lack of need for the products that result. This argument appeals to people who attempt to discriminate between the purposes for which animals suffer and die. It should not make much difference to the hard-liners who most cared for Ms Eagle's bill, and is in any case deeply flawed in the case of fur.

To stigmatise the fur trade efficiently, one would ideally need to demonstrate that it caused more suffering to animals than the other practices one stigmatised less, or prove that it was so egregiously, exceptionally, grievously extravagant that though it caused little suffering it could not be condoned.

Chapter Two deals with the issue of animal suffering and suggests that it is surprisingly small in the case of producing fur. One might bend over backwards and concede for the purposes of argument that mink and pig are on a par when it comes to the degree of their suffering or otherwise on farms. But what is as interesting is that it is the very arguments of vegetarianism and

---

[4] For such an argument see Scruton, 1996

veganism which help us see that the fur trade is really no more unnecessary than is the production of meat, milk or any other animal product. Marie Eagle's 'luxury' argument limps even more dramatically than does her 'welfare' argument.

It is demonstrably true that western man has no need of animal produce. We can eat a vegan diet without suffering. Indeed if the world fed less of its plant material to animals for human consumption, it would theoretically better support a large human population (Leach, 1976). There is even a case to be made that Westerners not only do not need to eat animal produce, but that they need to eat less of it. This is to say that over-consumption of animal produce shortens or worsens our lives. So one might say that a good deal of whatever suffering is involved in animal farming is not merely not useful to man, but produces human as well as animal suffering.

Maria Eagle's bill invoked a calculus of animal suffering versus human benefit, and supposed quite wrongly that it caught fur squarely in its net. Actually, her calculus would exonerate fur but trap the bacon sandwich or the pint of milk far more effectively. Or rather, it would trap the third bacon sandwich of the week, and the second ice cream. It would certainly trap the bulk of food animal production, even if it only slightly dented the principle of it.

## Changing Attitudes to Fur

There is no need to accept the argument about luxury in the terms those such as Maria Eagle, in common with most of the animal rights protesters, see it. True, fur has since the beginning of history been a symbol of affluence and display. From the medieval period until now, it was incorporated in ceremonial and official dress for that reason. Ermine, especially, has always been associated with authority. These habits and ideas probably flowed from the costliness of fabrics which were efficiently warm, but which above all had the same sort of exotic rarity value that attached to spices. They came, similarly, from far afield. They came through the entrepreneurship and courage of traders.

Fur has been fashionable in various periods ever since, perhaps especially in the last decades of the nineteenth century and the early decades of the twentieth century. It is hard at this distance to know what people thought then about the animals which had been killed to create the clothes they longed for. In the first decades of this century, far more fur came from trapped animals than was farmed. Farmed fur was not common until the 1930's. Whether people were just less interested in animal welfare then is hard to say. Certainly, the fate of an animal depended on its owner, since animals were conceived of as a person's property, and his rights over his property were sacred (Brown, 1974). They were less squeamish times, but arguably not much less caring or gentle for all that (Thomas, 1984). Human relations, too, were conducted with less superficial display of compassion, but arguably with just as great real or effective concern.

After the Second World War, furs remained the prerogative of old money, but they became in the 1950s, as they had been in the 30s, a piece of display desired by the new rich of show business and industry. This changed as protest began to make fur wearing in the US and northern Europe an increasingly confrontational and nerve-wracking business in the late 70s and throughout the 80s.

It must have seemed then to the protesters that the entire social scene had changed and moved in their favour. By the early 80s, Greenpeace was able to commission David Bailey to make the notorious cinema advertisement, with the slogan about many dumb animals giving up their lives to clothe just one dumb human animal. Many in the fashion and entertainment industries - models and ex-models amongst them - signed up to help make fur-wearing a despised habit. In 1995 Naomi Campbell famously aligned herself with the PETA (People for the Ethical Treatment of Animals) poster campaign in which naked models were photographed with the caption: 'We'd rather go naked than wear fur'. Apparently untroubled by her inconsistency, in 1997 and again in 1999 she was starring in catwalk shows featuring fur (Guardian, 1997; The Express, 1999).

Curiously, and unexpectedly, the protest, mostly based in England and the US, affected the trade much less than the campaigners supposed. The world economy was in recession for some of the period, and that, far more than the effect of protest, damaged the trade. Abroad, the protest had hardly any impact. In the UK, where there was impact, the market was and is too small to make very much difference to fur trade interests.

About 60 percent of the world trade in fur skins, but nothing like that proportion of the manufacture or retailing of fur garments, is conducted in London, always the centre of protest. This is a historical accident which flows from the exodus of Jewish fur dealers (they were almost never fur trappers) from continental Europe in the 1930s. They gravitated to England partly because the Hudson's Bay Company held huge fur auctions here then, and partly because there was then a Jewish manufacturing tradition here. A distinguished example of this phenomenon was the late J G Links, descended from a Hungarian immigrant furrier, he went on to earn the Royal Warrant, to become the holder of the medieval title, Furrier to the Queen, and was the author of books on fur. Joe Links was also a thriller writer, an authoritative art historian, and author of one of the century's most famous guides to Venice (*The Times*, 1997; *Daily Telegraph*, 1997). Now, however, there is hardly any garment manufacture in the UK.

It follows from all these factors that little might change if fur could no longer be farmed in the UK. Though there is evidence of scattered protest almost everywhere, including Norway where even whaling is widely tolerated, there is little prospect of the practice being banned elsewhere. So the contribution of the UK farmers would merely be made up elsewhere. The trade being an international one, fur farming is one of the few British agricultural practices which is almost entirely an export trade.

It is also useful to note that the UK retail trade for fur is tiny compared with its overseas counterparts, and the UK merchants depend on it very little. Protest might, at least conceivably, so depress fur wearing here that the tiny specialist retail trade disappeared. None of this would dent the vast majority of the fur trade's UK turnover. There would be a small but important dent in the UK export figures, however, since much of the English retail trade is in effect for re-export.

Fur, mostly from overseas, is traded through London offices, to manufacturers overseas, and imported here as garments for resale to customers perhaps half of whom are visitors to the UK and will take the goods home after their trip. Even when protest made trading difficult in the UK, the new rich of the Middle East, Asia and Russia in their turn brought new customers to the business.

## The Benefits of an Extravagant Trade

It might not matter to the protesters, but the majority of UK farmed fur goes into a trade whose main feature is that it takes a noisome waste product of the meat and food industries and turns it into a luxury export. This is in fact in several ways the least wasteful of all uses of animals. The mink farm takes food waste, for instance, from abattoirs and cereals manufacturers, most of which could not go into the human food chain, and turns it into fur and useful products (Rouvinen, 1999). The fur is obviously valued. But even the meat and bone of a dead mink are usually not wasted: the dead bodies are usually sent to renders, where their fat makes a prized oil. The manure of the living animals is valued by farmers.

The fur trade has occasionally justified its existence by stressing that fur is an ecologically sound means of keeping warm, and have hoped by this argument to suggest that fur answers basic human needs. This reasoning is sound so far as it goes, but it does not quite go far enough.

There are all sorts of ways of keeping warm, but the one we should really celebrate is the one which satisfies one of the greatest of human urges: the urge to extravagance. The dislike of luxury which lies behind much anti-fur protest ignores the fact that luxury is vital to human society, and that this form of extravagance comes without the ecological disadvantage which attaches to, say, the ownership and use of large cars or speedboats, or even to foreign travel by jet plane.

There is a powerful case to be made for the idea that the need for luxury is one of the most fundamental human urges, as it is one of the most powerful well-springs of activity in the whole animal kingdom. Biologists have long understood a Darwinian explanation for the apparent excesses of display indulged in by animals such as the peacock. Sexual attractiveness that involves a conspicuous and costly display demonstrates a male's ability to satisfy to an extraordinary degree the capacity to fulfil his basic needs.

Jared Diamond, Professor of Physiology at the University of California, Los Angeles and a leading evolutionary biologist, cites the views of various biologists to the effect that conspicuous display is useful to animals perhaps because their capacity to survive whilst throwing huge resources at display promises genetic success (Diamond, 1997).

But what about people, with their subtler and more powerful minds? Professor Diamond supposes that our attitude to adornment and display may always have had something in common with the adaptive behaviour of animals. He compares and contrasts a stag's antlers with a piece of human display common in the West:

> (a stag's antlers represent an). investment of calcium, phosphate, and calories, yet they are grown and discarded each year. Only the most well-nourished males - ones that are mature, socially dominant, and free of parasites - can afford that investment. Hence a female deer can regard big antlers as an honest ad for male quality, just as a woman whose boyfriend buys and discards a Porsche sports car each year can believe his claim of being wealthy. But antlers carry a second message not shared with Porsches. Whereas a Porsche does not generate more wealth, big antlers do bring their owner access to the best pastures by enabling him to defeat rival males and fight off predators.

Actually, the Porsche does bear at least a passing relationship to utility. Throughout history, men have needed to be swift. Even in historically recent times they have needed to be well-mounted. The quality and expense of a man's horse was a sign to himself and others he sought to impress that he had glamorous and extravagant as well as efficient means of locomotion. The horse's modern replacement and surrogate is the sports car. True, for most forms of getting about, a Porsche is not a highly functional piece of equipment, but it can function as a necessary car for most purposes, more or less.

In any case, redundancy is also important, in human affairs as in nature, as Professor Diamond reminds us:

> While any man can boast to a woman that he is rich and therefore she should go to bed with him in the hopes of enticing him into marriage, he might be lying. Only when she sees him throwing away money on useless expensive jewellery and sports cars can she believe him.

This sort of argument has been retailed elegantly by Geoffrey Miller, who cites the Israeli biologist Amotz Zahavi's 'The Handicap Principle' to the effect that 'there is a necessary tension between natural selection (for survival) and sexual selection (for attracting mates), and waste is at the heart of that tension.... The Handicap Principle suggests that prodigious waste is a necessary feature of sexual courtship.' Humans, like animals, expend energy and wealth in evidencing their attractiveness as gene-stock. They do so as part of their instinctual make-up. They flourish when they can display well, and suffer when they cannot (Miller, 1999).

Modern consumer society operates on the principle that conspicuous consumption may pose moral dilemmas, of course it does, but that it is nevertheless an important engine of human happiness and well-being. That is why few of us condemn the quest for glamour. Fur is not merely an extravagant item of display, it is an overtly sexual one. This is the essence of glamour: it is where power, money and sexuality meet. Glamour cannot really be polite, understated, modest. It has some difficulty hanging on to being merely decent. Liz Hurley characterises modern British glamour: she wears expensive clothes and diamonds and is perhaps beautiful. But she is in the image of Diana Dors, say, in outrageous and overt sexual immodesty.

Glamour cannot really operate in private. Though the ownership, say, of Fendi furs or Ferraris, is essentially an egotistical matter, it is only a very eccentric person who enjoys these goods in private. Their public display is crucial to their enjoyment.

The interesting thing about this element of public display of these sorts of goods is that to a surprising degree, the rest of us get a free ride from their ownership by others. Our magazines and television are enlivened, let alone largely paid for, by the blandishments of advertisers enticing the rich; the fashion and society pages and gossip columns all shower us with examples of the luxury and attractiveness of the rich and their spending. We can ogle the images of what we cannot afford. If we have the good sense to keep envy and jealousy in their place, we can enjoy the fantasy without too much resentment.

There is a strand of Christian thinking which disparages this sort of display, and the vicarious pleasure we may take in it, as worldly, unspiritual, egotistical, and which instead celebrates abstemiousness as being in the tradition of asceticism of the founding fathers of the faith. This tendency has underpinned socialism from its medieval beginnings, and it now permeates green thinking, which prides itself on reducing man's impact on nature and countering materialism.

Whatever the apparent value of the pedigree of worries about materialism, it has several difficulties. One is that it does not allow for the facts of human nature. But another is that it is hard to decouple the great moral value of the free economy and the free society from their roots in individualism, and that by definition is not amenable to discipline.

Capitalism is the business of harnessing the aspirations to affluence, display and glamour as basic energising forces for the entire economy. Capitalism has the merit of encouraging and rewarding the accumulation of wealth, and of channelling the energies of powerful people into acquiring and displaying wealth whilst creating opportunities and affluence all around them. It rewards risk-taking with wealth, and freely celebrates the channelling of wealth into waste and glamour (North, 1999). So far as we know, societies which stifle these opportunities for very long develop covert consumption and status-seeking by elites which are either criminal or state-sponsored.

So we need to see the social merit of conspicuous consumption by individuals. It satisfies those who are successfully ambitious and spurs on those who are merely ambitious, while it diverts society at large.

One could go so far as to say that one of the great merits of the fur trade is that it precisely is a luxury trade, satisfying not the boringly basic human needs, but far more interesting and vital ones. In an important way, wants are needs. A society which cannot give people what they want, will pall. It will pall in interest and vibrancy, but it will also soon more seriously fail to attract or keep some of the most useful of its citizens. A society that cannot entice the few cannot sustain the many.

These arguments should not be contentious in an age which has rejected socialism. They remain so because populism dictates a slight anxiety about anything which might be called elitism.

*Bien pensant* opinion mostly affects to despise the matter of getting rich, though liberal-minded writers and artists, or liberal lawyers, are no less dedicated to getting wealth than their right-wing counterparts. Still, the aesthetic of the intelligentsia tends toward understated means of expressing their financial well-being, and eschews the flashily vulgar expenditure of those who are inventing new ways of making money.

Wearing furs now hovers between two interesting extremes, rather as does the ownership of Rolls Royces. It is the preserve alike of those with old money who are damned if they should give up old ways of displaying it, and of those with new money who are not yet abashed about vulgar display.

It would be a bleak prospect for stylish UK and other European fashion (or motorcar) retailers, if they believed their domestic market to be either fusty or flashy. And one might think that there was worse news to come for the purveyors of a luxury product devoted to glamour. Surely they should be suffering in an age when a kind of nihilistic scruffiness and minimalist expensiveness has become the height of fashion?

Oddly, though, after years in which it seemed that the opinion-formers in the fashion world were going along with the protesters, and adopting a certain protest chic (think of designer houses like Red Or Dead or Katherine Hamnett), there is now strong evidence that old-fashioned glamour, and fur in particular, have proved capable of attracting a new generation of designers and customers.

Luxury for its own sake is in fashion, even after being discredited by the downfall of the yuppies and the Trumps (briefly), and after satirical successes such as Tom Wolfe's *Bonfire Of the Vanities*. Now we see the downmarket film, Diamonds Are Forever, being celebrated by the diamond industry (formerly a South African pariah), and by a galaxy of minor stars in borrowed diamonds, all given the blessing of Prince Charles sporting a Versace handkerchief in his breast pocket.

Fur in particular has flourished because the idea of glamour has certain constants. But fur also has newer connotations which have found their way into fashion.

## Modernism

The modern mind is not easy to chart. But one thing seems especially to characterise it. It dislikes rules. Many of the customers for fur retailers are now young women who have made their own way and their own money, and if they want sports cars and furs, that is exactly what they will have. They do not need the say-so of socialist or green or animal rights people to tell them whether such expenditure is acceptable. They are not interested in liberal opinion. This generation of young women will indulge its instincts with scant respect for respectability, or, at the extreme, even the law.

One strand of these instincts is rather similar to the strand of 'dangerous' Romanticism which the Age of Reason, the Enlightenment, spawned in Britain at the birth of the 'Modern': say around the beginning of the 19th Century (Johnson, 1991). The wild became interesting, and many people liked to be counted amongst, or yearned to be, 'mad, bad and dangerous to know', as Lady Caroline Lamb described Lord Byron after their first meeting in 1812. Indeed, the *farouche* nature of the fashionable and Bohemian world has much in common with the thoughtless extremism of those who protest against what they see as its greatest excess: fur-wearing. Both pit their own right to extreme behaviour against the conventional decencies of boring bourgeois society.

It is interesting that many modern artists are addressing the issue of man's relations with his own body, dead or alive, and with animals. The latter are not seen from a bunny-hugging, animal rights point of view. Much of the work of people like Damien Hirst is a meditation on animals and our feelings about them which has anything but an animal rights perspective. After all, Damien Hirst himself is a co-proprietor of restaurants which sell animal produce at high prices. Charles Saatchi, patron of modern art and, according to one paper, 'the creator of New Neurotic Realism', plans to turn his controversial Royal Academy of Arts show, Sensation, into a theme for a string of restaurants in which, 'diners can expect to sit amongst.... A shark in formaldehyde by Hirst...' (*Sunday Telegraph*, 1999).

Fur takes its place in this new aesthetic. Its appeal is an atavistic one. In wearing fur one is in the tradition of one's earliest hunting forebears, and of one's medieval ancestors. The new catwalk style of fur is not *soignée*, it is savage. Its most distinctive feature is to use fur as though the wearer were a Neanderthal tribes woman, and the fur itself is made to seem as though it were hot from the animal's back. This actually belies the way that it is modern, highly technical, treatment of fur which allows such freedom of use (*Daily Telegraph*, 1999).

There is no contradiction, and nothing new, in this deliberate anachronism and atavism. Styles in food, furniture and fashion are always driven forward as much by admiration for the peasant and the primitive as for the sophisticated. Like much that is truly stylish, fur demonstrates how the primitive and the sophisticated are in close proximity. The revival of fur in the fashion trade comes about as part of an interest in the primitive, even the warrior and certainly the hunting heritage. Without thinking it through, designers are drifting toward the Romantic, the gothic and the medieval for inspiration, and fur finds its place in that aesthetic as attractive, but dangerous too.

The whole world of the arts is now, as it has always been, infected by an urge which seeks to break down barriers of any sort. As soon as we think we have understood what certain people will think and feel, we find that a dynamic society overturns the cliché.

We might, for instance, note that the Institute of Contemporary Art is now headed by Ivan Massow, a commercially-successful homosexual master of fox hounds (*Daily Telegraph*, 1999a). This is a confluence of four attributes and activities (art, entrepreneurship, overt homosexuality, hunting) which even a decade ago would be unlikely to co-habit. It is of a piece with an almost anarchic melt-down of old patterns of thought, of old ideas of decency.

Designers and their customers are not making political statements when using fur. Nonetheless in the present climate it takes a certain courage to buy and wear fur. Fur-wearing takes its place with other new patterns in fashion because it is challenging, and defiant. It is dissident, but not in the old way: it is not cocking a snook at the old Establishment (as dissidence used to seek to do). It is cocking a snook against the newly established political correctness of the left and of the greens. Aristocrats, country people, parvenus, artists and designers can ally on that, if on little else. Like any true social change, it is not just a matter of poses, but of muddles of attributes rearranging themselves in people's minds. It is much more a question of what people are allowing themselves to say or do than of any deep change in what they actually are. It is not a change in what people want, but in what they admit to, allow or expect.

It is no use applying ordinary standards of moral seriousness to fashion, any more than it is useful to apply them to art. The most serious artist, like the fashion designer, will always be tempted to test a prohibition, rather as he or she will always test an inhibition, to see if this is an area in which a shock and a surprise can be delivered. People do not ask permission from moralists before finding something compelling. When people want to take risks, live dangerously, or explore this or that aspect of taste, they do so often in defiance of respectable, intelligent or compassionate opinion. This is not to say that wearing fur is irrational or hard-hearted: it is merely to say that a charge of irrationality or even cruelty might not deter people from wanting to do it. And so fur, because of who dislikes it, is bound to attract new friends. Socially, nothing attracts like opposition.

Without permission from respectable opinion, and in defiance of what might have been thought to be settled objections, and quite contrary to expectation, designers and customers are swinging toward increasing use of fur. The catwalks are full of it, though usually in the form of trims and accessories. Young designers are spearheading the most avant-garde explorations of this new vogue. Models (most notably Naomi Campbell) who previously, and probably thoughtlessly, had opined that fur was unspeakably cruel, now seem happy to wear it.

But it would be a mistake to see the switch to fur as a political statement in itself. *The Economist* has noted the recent flurry of interest in fur and concluded that the return to fur is not self-consciously political. 'For the last word, however, it makes sense to go to the designers, and they have a rather less complicated take on the subject. According to Jean-Paul Gaultier, 'It is not about politics, it is about quality. If you want the softness and lightness and warmth of skin, you use skin. Nothing feels like sable. If you want that feeling, you use that ..... There was a lot of fur in the autumn/winter couture shows because the couturiers had suddenly remembered that in autumn/winter, in the northern hemisphere, fur is, well - nice.' (*The Economist*, 1999). What is more, the tendency toward the outrageous and the animal is not being driven by cynical and case-hardened older gurus and trend-setters. Rather, the old guard makes regular pilgrimages to the graduation shows of places such as St Martin's College of Fashion in London, whose alumni are reported to be driven much more by a quest for freshness, feel and theatricality than they are by any self-consciously serious ideas (*Evening Standard*, 1999). This is not a case of Reactionary Chic, the successor to Radical Chic.

Those who once opposed fur have not necessarily rethought the issue. The support for fur of some of the people who now work in or model it is not necessarily comforting to the trade merely because they once opposed the trade. There is no sign that many of them did much thinking when they condemned fur, and their reinstatement of it does not seem either to have flowed from fresh study or research. They do not seem so much to have changed their mind as merely their behaviour. They have not so much adapted their moral thinking as reconsidered what is fashionable.

This shades into the political only when one remembers that there is a strong modern imperative to the permissive. There is a spirit of aggressive pluralism in the air. This is very testing to those whose business is pressing for bans, and it is hardly less so for those who press for a courteous understanding of other people's sensitivity. In all sorts of respects, we seem to be seeing a reaction to the 'ban' culture, as we do to the 'blame' culture. It is not merely the right which dislikes both: in the permissive and libertarian LM magazine, the left too has discovered the joys of choice.

At its least attractive this is manifest in people's impatience with any restriction on their behaviour, as when, for instance, jet-skiers speed dangerously and noisily close to swimmers, or youngsters allow their stereos to 'leak' into the hearing of everyone else sharing a railway carriage with them. It is quite funny, when it is seen as young people defiantly smoking in the street, and less so when they do it in the Tube. When the outrageous behaviour is risky or costly only to the perpetrator, we surely ought to reach over backwards to condone it.

But what happens when desires compete noisily or dangerously? What are we to say when we are up against what Ivan Illich called the 'radical monopoly': for instance, when someone seeking quiet is afflicted with the tyranny, as he sees it, of noise? What are we to say when a young man's enterprise brings him to busk in our train, and pits his love of his own voice against our expectation of a normal silence? Or when he shoves the Big Issue in your face, or she her baby? Or when an overweight middle aged man arrives in the supermarket wearing a sleeveless vest? Or, to come to our issue, what to make about the woman in fur who stands between two vegans in the supermarket queue? These are all forms of social pollution, so far as those who do not like them are concerned. How to unpick these problems?

We cannot give in to a tyranny of the sensitive. A man has the right to smell of beer on the tube; we cannot stop people wearing shell-suits. We cannot make public places subject themselves to a fascism of orderliness. Few vegans are so sensitive that they could not eat a veggie-burger in a McDonald's, where others celebrate the muscle of beef, the breast and leg of chicken. Surely, people have a right to wear fur in public and still be the subject of the more normal rules of politeness.

However, it is no use to say that the wearing of fur is no-one's business but the furrier's and their customers. There is a moral dimension to fur wearing, whatever the indifference of many fur-designers or fur-wearers to the lives and deaths of fur-bearers. It is entirely possible that a strong body of modern opinion may support people's right to take pleasure in animals any way they like. This would not make such use or consumption right. It might even make it all the more important that people who were interested in animals take all the more interest.

The problem is not unique to fur by any means. We have seen in many areas of intensive husbandry that many consumers simply buy on price, and it has really fallen to a minority to consider the animals' welfare or indeed to consider the animal at all. As Stephen Budiansky notes in The Covenant of the Wild, modern society seems schizophrenically composed of people who treat animals as humans and those who treat them as things. The latter might well be the case with some fur-wearers (Budiansky, 1994).

It might seem odd that people who wear fur are not often interested in how the animal who contributed to the product came to do so. One might think that consumers for fur would like to know whether it was trapped in the high arctic, or farmed in

Scandinavia. But that is how it is, and the matter is much the same with people eating bacon or beef.

People have the right to wear fur without thinking about animals at all, if that is what they want to do. There is no form of human consumption of legal goods and services which requires that one consider the wider dimensions of what one does. The Rolls Royce owner is not obliged to understand enough atmospheric physics to determine whether his threat to global warming is too great to be tolerated. The McDonald's customer does not have to wonder about the cow that made his meat. The girl getting engaged does not have to wonder how many black South Africans burrowed miles below the earth's surface for her gem.

These are matters which anyone can take an interest in, and it is probably well that some people do. But we are not all required to, and actually could not. Pressure groups exist to try to force their particular agenda on to society, and they do a useful job in attempting to keep us up to the mark. But that does not make them right when they target selected, highly personalised, villains (say, customers of fur shops) rather than address the political process as to whether an activity (say, fur-wearing) ought to be proscribed. Besides, their energetic espousal of this or that view does not have a particularly firm grasp of rectitude merely because it is committed and dedicated. When pressure groups pit themselves against interest groups, it is almost always forgotten that they have vested interests too. Society is entitled to be sceptical, lackadaisical, traditional, and permissive in face of their reforming zeal. This is not purely a matter of laziness: the committed and the partisan are often wrong and narrow-minded, as well as dogmatic. The rest of society is entitled to apply a leisurely scepticism to their urgency.

These are the sorts of reasons why it was odd that in Beverly Hills recently there was a proposal that fur products should be labelled as having been killed by such means as gassing, electrocution and neck wringing. Down that road madness lies. Firstly, the reality of such things is not conveyed by a couple of words; secondly, the list ranges from the innocuous to the tortured, and of the item in one's hand, one would have no way of knowing which applied. Thirdly, to be just, such a stigmatisation would need to be applied to all animal produce, of which the label would be equally true, and equally misleading.

## The Specious Claims of Anti-fur Agitation

The protesters make various claims about the popularity of fur which appear incontrovertible, but which are deeply flawed. They cunningly claim that 'the fur trade is a dying trade',[5] when actually it is merely one with ups and downs, and currently a thriving world wide market (see Table 1). What is more, they claim that the public is drifting away from fur of its own accord. But there is good anecdotal evidence that those women who now own furs would mostly have gone on enjoyably wearing them if they had not felt castigated and endangered as they did so. This is important. Fur wearing has remained attractive to those who knew and liked it: they have been intimidated - not persuaded - out of wearing what they want. The anti-fur protesters need to be seen as people who have bullied people, but not won their minds. What is more, it is not true, as is routinely claimed by protesters, that retailers ceased stocking fur because it had become unpopular and unprofitable. For instance, there is evidence in correspondence from Harrods that the store ceased to stock fur because it had succumbed to intolerable animal rights pressure, and the threat of damage and possibly violence it brought.[6] This in spite of public protestations to the contrary.

So far from society having drifted away from fur because arguments were presented to it, actually women who were enjoying buying and wearing fur were forced to stop wearing it because they had been robbed of the pleasure of the thing, and had

---

[5] see Table 1.

[6] I have seen letters written by Harrods' management insisting that its fur business was profitable, but that protest against it brought intolerable pressure on the store. This is quite at odds with Harrods' public stance that it would never give into pressure.

nastiness imposed instead. Wearing fur went from being a luxury to being at least unpleasant and quite possibly a danger.

The events of the past decade or so have left the protesters believing that they have in effect won the argument, if not yet finally been successful in driving the fur trade to extinction. In truth, the argument has barely begun.

Public opinion polls are often cited as proving that the public has a settled attitude of antagonism to the fur trade (Eagle, 1999). But in so far as this implies that the majority of British people dislike the trade, this only means that a large number of people very ignorant of and thoughtless about an issue has a firm view of it.

After all, the majority of people are either wholly ignorant of the issue or in receipt of only one side of the argument. There is good evidence that once they are more informed, instincts of fair play seem to take opinion in rather different directions. It is especially noteworthy that when a jury, picked to be representative of society at large, heard both sides of the argument for a television show it voted seven to five in favour of the 'accused', a fur-farmer pleading to be allowed to continue his trade (Widdecombe, 1998). Both sides of the argument had been put, fairly and squarely. What may have persuaded the jury above all was that the fur-farmer was patently an ordinary Briton, who seemed likely to be speaking the truth when he said he liked his animals the way any farmer likes his charges, and would not knowingly harm them. This may well have been an efficient reality-check for the jury.

The change of view once the 'jury' has real evidence, or a rounder context is a common phenomenon. There is good evidence that people are suspicious about things about which they hear in the media (the NHS in general, the water industry in general, politicians in general) but much more positive about what they actually know (their doctor or hospital, their water provider, their own MP). Similarly, there is good evidence that asking the question, 'Should scientists be allowed to experiment on animals?', received a very different response from people asked it 'cold' and those asked a 'warm start' version which included the condition:

Some scientists are developing and testing new drugs to reduce pain... animal experiments.... make more rapid progress (possible).'. When asked the question cold, 'Just 24 per cent of people were in favour, with 64 per cent against... On the 'warm start' question people backed animal experimentation by a slim majority, with 45 per cent for, versus 41 against... a swing of 22 percent'. Interestingly, only two per cent of those polled had worn a fur coat or pursued blood sports, but 62 per cent of this group clearly favoured animal experimentation: arguably, their realism was allied with robust humanitarianism (*New Scientist*, 1999).

All this leaves protesters in a peculiar position. The most ardent protesters are almost universally from the left, though many of their less active but occasionally vocal supporters are not. The hard core had thought to have the argument going almost exclusively their way. There were and are few voices raised in defence of the fur trade. And yet the trade remains robust and capable of winning votes in favour of its survival when it gets a decent hearing.

The media has never bothered to provide that hearing. Fur has been discussed almost entirely, when it has achieved coverage at all, in terms of its fashion interest and on fashion pages. These have occasionally ventured into the issue and usually done so from a profoundly biased anti-fur point of view. When fur has been in the news at the front of newspapers, it has been so mostly when anti-fur protesters managed a stunt which seemed worthy of note in its own right.

The media is seldom interested in the business of balanced reporting in the issues it covers. It is most comfortable with the views of campaign and protest groups which seem intuitively to be on the side of the angels and to express the views of 'the people' and their thinking. Business, by contrast, gets short shrift, as does science. On the other hand, if one is patient, most issues will receive the coverage they deserve. The media has other instincts than its socially and politically dissident attitudes. It has a low boredom threshold and will in the end tire of almost any attitude it adopts. It loves surprises. It also has a taste for the underdog. And then there is the competitive spirit of the media: no attitude which appeals to the left or liberal world will for long be popular in the right-wing press, and vice versa.

Thus, every position, and every inclination, of the journalist is in constant turmoil, and under constant fire and threat of overthrow. Greenpeace, for instance, has long been one of the media's heroes, accepted on all sides as a source of good images, stirring stories, and populist comment. But that did not protect the campaigners from criticism when the media began to perceive them as over-mighty.

In the end, Shell's point of view over Brent Spar did begin to come through, and Greenpeace's apparent triumph turned to dust as the media turned on it. In the end, an honest reading of the BSE risk has been filtering through. Already, about three months after it first hit the headlines, the media is beginning to see that Monsanto's point of view on GMOs may be at least as respectable as Greenpeace's (North, forthcoming).

There is a detectable pattern to how these events unfold. Greenpeace's victory over Shell, for example, prompted journalists to wonder whether the campaigners' power was legitimate and to look for the first time with some sympathy at Shell's position.

In the case of fur, by far the best coverage the industry had ever received occurred when campaigners broke into fur farms and released thousands of mink into the wild, in the New Forest August 1998 and on the Staffordshire/Shropshire border in September 1998. Suddenly, the plight of the animals and the danger they posed to indigenous wildlife made journalists wonder whether the protesters were necessarily right. Writers from the *Daily Telegraph* and *The Times* were for the first time despatched to write about the actualities of the farms rather than the myths perpetuated by campaigners (*The Times*, 1998a; *Daily Telegraph*, 1998; *The Times* 1998b). The reports were by and large favourable. The journalists were perhaps surprised, but also seemingly impressed, by the normality of the farms they saw. The next burst of favourable coverage happened when Maria Eagle launched her Bill (*The Times*, 1999a, *Daily Telegraph*, 1999c)..

Most recently, the trend has continued as the Government announced its bill (*The Times* 1999f).

# 2. The Animals

Goodness knows, finally, by what right mankind uses animals. Religious people may feel they do so under some sort of license from the deity. The rest of us have to come to some more obviously rational explanation. This is not the place for a long discussion of the moral underpinnings for the human use of animals, fascinating as that might be. What does matter here is to discus whether the use of animals for their fur is any worse than the use of animals for anything else. We are not arguing that fur-farming is especially virtuous, but that it bears strict comparison with many other forms of animal use we do not condemn half as much. We dare to go a little further: fur farming does not seem to cause undue suffering by any of the rather good means humans have developed to think about such things.

Millions of animals die every year to provide fur. About 85 per cent of them will have been raised in farms. About 85 per cent of the animals will be mink, and of those about 85 percent will have been raised on farms, the vast majority of them in Denmark, and rather fewer in Holland and north America. A very few of these 30 million or so farmed mink - perhaps 120,000 - will have been raised in the UK. Of the fur-bearers, only mink are raised in the UK. A handful of other species are raised in small numbers on farms in other countries. The big majority of these non-mink animals are foxes of various breeds, and most of those are raised in Finland and Norway.

One advantage of the concentration of fur-farming in these old and affluent northern democracies is that the vast majority of animals farmed for fur live and die in countries with law-abiding farmers who are inspected by organised and thorough ministerial watchdogs. This is not mostly a cowboy business.

It does, however, have its ugly side. I do not mean that there is the necessity of killing the animals. We will come to the apparently grim side of even good farming. What matters here is that animal rights campaigners have been able to find a few examples of manifestly bad and sometimes criminally poor farming. This is almost all the general pubic knows of fur-farming: blurred videos and impassioned denunciations are all they had to go on.

So far as I know, the campaigners have no evidence of bad farming in continental Europe, nor of widespread abuses anywhere. But Stella McCartney, for instance, has done the voice-over for a PETA (People for the Ethical Treatment of Animals) video which was sent to many fashion designers who have had the temerity to use fur. The footage purported to show foxes, and other animals, on a US fur farm, and many of the animals seemed very obviously to be in an appalling state of neglect. The BFTA insist that this was not actually a fur farm at all.[7]

Nearer home, Respect For Animals obtained footage, apparently in England, of mink in a state of excitement, and perhaps of stress. This video was shown by Maria Eagle at a press conference to launch her private member's bill to ban fur farming, and snippets of it have been widely seen on British television. The animals are seen to rush about their cages, clearly agitated. The difficulty, however, is that the place involved is not identified. The animals might conceivably have been on a farm (it would have been a very unusual as well as a regrettable one) on which animals were routinely stressed and in need of help. But the material might have been obtained by first deliberately exciting the animals and them filming the resulting chaos. Respect has video of disturbed animals on a southern England mink farm: but the British Fur Trade Association insists the material dates from

---

[7] PETA claimed the video showed conditions on a fox farm in Illinois – in fact the farmer named was not a fur farmer at all, but a scent farmer – the animals shown on the video, including racoons, were all taken from the wild, whereas foxes farmed in US are from breeding stock going back more than 70 generations. Another pointer is that racoons are not farmed for their fur and yet the video clearly showed racoons in cages. Finn racoons are farmed in Europe but they are a different species from the racoon even though they have more or less the same name. Finn racoons are from the canine family.

the chaotic months following releases of the animals by rights activists. The careful pairing of animals, and their entire way of life, was hugely disrupted and their behaviour on being forcibly reunited and grouped with animals they did not know was predictably vicious and confused.

Respect have filmed a worker on one of England's 13 mink farms: it was footage which led to the man's being charged and convicted on several counts of animal abuse in 1999. He was shown swinging an animal through the air as it hung on to his hand by its teeth. This was valuable and depressing information, so far as it went and may amount to the only socially valuable work Respect has done.

At the worst it proved that a farmer might be a member of the small British Fur Breeder's Association and not adhere to adequate standards of staff management. The association's farmer-officials were duly and rightly shocked and claim to have taken tighter control on matters. As representatives of ten of the 11 licensed fur farmers, perhaps they were remiss not to have been more rigorous, earlier.

Beyond that, the film possibly demonstrated that it is quite easy to do mink farming very badly, as it is easy to do any farming badly. It is also entirely possible, and highly profitable, to do mink farming well. This latter is not easy, but then no intensive husbandry is easy. It would not be the first thought for someone seeking a quick buck. Indeed, the country's two leading fur-farmers have told me they enjoyed mink-keeping since childhood, in very much the way another country-dweller might enjoy keeping ferrets. They may have proved canny hobbyists, but their trade began with the affection for their charges which characterises a hobby.

## The Realities of Fur Farming

There are few British fur farmers, but several of them have taken interested neighbours and media around their farms. The most persistently bold of these is Mike Cobbledick, of Cornwall, who has received the same sort of attention from protesters as most fur farmers, but has remained the most publicly unabashed and bullish about the quality of his work and the well-being of his animals. To that end, he allowed TV cameras on to his farm right at the height of the furore over Maria Eagle's bill to ban his sort of husbandry. The resulting footage was seen on BBC's Countryfile and on Sky News and showed serried ranks of cages in airy open low sheds and within each cage, breeding mink looking lively, relaxed, inquisitive, as they usually do on well-run farms. Rather similar footage was shown on West Eye View, an HTV series (which also gave an outing to the Respect footage discussed above). Had the cameras lingered, they might have been able to catch the animals showing clear irritation and perhaps even fear: mink do not like their territory for long being invaded by humans, however friendly. At the right time of year, female mink could be shown with the annual average of five young, rather more than they could expect in the wild, so fit are they. The males could be seen grown to about twice their average weight in the wild. Quite possibility their longevity would also be increased in captivity, though that is not proven. If it were, that would complete the triumvirate of advantages (fertility, healthiness and longevity), which are normally conferred on creatures in well-managed captivity.

It is always easy to portray caged animals as resentful, suffering and oppressed. The sight of wire alone will do that. Add to that the fact that mink cages are not for long shiny and smart, but mildly grubby, and one has a ready source of worrying images. But the footage from Mike Cobbledick's farm goes a long way to reassure that on the face of it mink are in good fettle.

Even so, impressions can be misleading. The disinterested observer has to look behind the TV images for something a little more rigorous as evidence. It may help that I have visited five mink farms and seen only evidence which supports the Cobbledick rather than the Respect view of what happens on well-managed farms. It is true that I have only seen farms whose owners were invited by the trade to show me round. They were farms the trade was proud of. Two were in England, and three in Denmark. Of the Danish farms, two were research stations. One of the enemies of mink farming, Professor Roger Harris of Bristol University's zoology department, has suggested to me in a telephone conversation that I might have been taken to farms just after feeding time when the animals were especially relaxed, and suggested that this would be an obvious ploy. But on reflection, I remember having seen animals being fed, which implies that I also saw them just before they were fed. This is the time when their behaviour is said to be most disturbing. Actually, I saw nothing odd. It is not unduly significant that observers may see only good farms: the case in favour of fur-farming needs to show that the thing can be well done and to accept that it should be done as well as it can be, not prove that it is always done well. Even my own impressions would not quite do as an indicator of animal welfare, even for my own satisfaction.

## Academic Studies

There is a good deal of academic research work on farmed mink welfare, and some of it is English, serious and recent. Much more of the work is Danish or Dutch. It comes from veterinary or zoological departments of established universities. None of it was sponsored directly by fur farm interests, though the trade has provided animals and facilities to some projects at home and abroad.[8] Some of the continental work was sponsored by state agriculture departments, who have a reputation for being as concerned with commercial interests as they are with abstract matters of animal welfare. However, even research sponsored by agriculture ministries has to survive peer review, and the workers in such university departments have to be scrupulous if they are to survive the implied taint which comes with their funding. It is sometimes claimed that one of the journals used by Continental scientists for their publications, *Scientifur*, is not adequately peer-reviewed. Actually, the most important insights contained in papers there are to be found from the same authors in peer-reviewed journals, so the point seems redundant.

---

[8] Telephone conversations and meeting with Knud Erik Heller, Associate Professor, Zoological Institute, University of Copenhagen, 1996-1999.

One strand of Dutch work, that of Professor P R Wiepkema in the 80s and 90s, and now followed on by Professor B M Spruijt, of the University of Utrecht, corrals the best evidence available to propose reforms in fur farming to the Dutch Minister of Agriculture, Nature Conservancy and Fisheries and the Dutch Parliament. In 1995, all the parties agreed a ten year Plan of Approach, or action plan (Wiepkema, 1994; Spruijt, 1999).

All of the researchers who conduct this work are respectable by any standards. Some believe that mink welfare is approaching acceptability, and is in any case not easy to improve. Most believe mink welfare to be amongst the best of any intensively farmed animal. Many hold this belief having worked with other farmed species, or having worked alongside others who do.

## Welfare Policies for Mink and Fox

This general view was clearly not held by the members of the Farm Animal Welfare Council, the British expert advisory panel whose studies and recommendations have formed the basis of Government efforts to improve conditions on animal farms since the 70s. This group produced a two page report on fur farming in 1989 (FAWC, 1989).. It said, 'Mink and fox have been bred in captivity for only about 50-60 generations and the Council is particularly concerned about the keeping of what are essentially wild animals in small barren cages.' But this was self-evidently a cursory survey, based on few farm visits and citing none of the available research, or experience, from abroad. Even so it did not condemn fur farming out of hand, but struck a decidedly sceptical note and asked for more research.

That seemed to be that. The UK fur-farmers suffered constant protest activities, and fewer and fewer remained in the business, partly depressed by the pressure against them and partly by low prices during the world economic downturn in the early 90s. The glamour and expense of fur did not suit the mood of a post-yuppy world in retreat from excess.

Ministry of Agriculture, Fisheries and Food (MAFF) vets continued to visit the gradually reducing numbers of fur farms, mostly to ensure that mink were kept in sufficient security and were slaughtered humanely. There was no intensive inspection of welfare matters, though the trade had entered into a voluntary agreement about cage sizes and other matters in the early 80s. The trade had also voluntarily invited inspection by respected vets, and sought to improve their standards in the light of the resulting reports (Kelsall, 1999). They have told the UK Ministry of Agriculture, Fisheries and Food that they could undertake to abide by the Dutch reform process, especially in exchange for a similar period of stability in which to make the necessary investments.[9]

The international development of policy toward fur farming has mostly taken place in the Council of Europe, which has corralled its member states in an agreement on guidelines for farmers. The latest Recommendation of the Standing Committee of the European Convention for the Protection of Animals Kept For Farming Purposes was adopted on 22 June 99. British agriculture officials have played a prominent role in the Council of Europe reform process, which makes it all the more paradoxical that the current government should be more interested in a ban than in reform, and not at all in a rational discussion of the issues.

## The Incoherency of Reform Proposals

Until recently, British non-specialist readers who wanted to understand mink welfare would have had no easy way into the research material. There was no bibliography which brought the material together. That was put right in 1997 by the Animal Welfare Information Centre of the School of Veterinary Medicine at Cambridge University. Commissioned by Respect, the Centre, headed by Donald Broom, the university's professor of animal welfare (his name is on the cover as having assisted the work), comprehensively trawled the literature and wrote a review of it.

The document mentions in several places various reforms to the existing cage system which might aid mink welfare, and then, incongruously, goes on to say that the existing cage system could not be reformed sufficiently to make welfare tolerable. Either of

---

[9] Letter from BFTA to MAFF, 9 December, 1998.

these propositions might be true or false, but the two cannot sensibly be sustained together.

The document might be taken as making a case for reforms far wider than the trade would enjoy, but that certainly does not make a case, nor does the document explicitly try to make a case, for banning mink farming.

It is as well that the Broom document has seldom been prayed in aid of the case for banning fur farming. It is altogether rather a poor piece of work. It reads more like a partisan effort of campaigning than a research document, or even a discussion document, which might have claims to be worthy of a great university. Its conclusions seem to be at odds with one another. It criticises the quality of much of the research on which it bases its own conclusions. It relies on research papers alone to reach conclusions which would have been far more credible had they been supported - or capable of support - by an element of real-life discussion with researchers, or visits to farms.

Nevertheless, the document does at least represent a comprehensive list of the available literature, and it charts pretty successfully the main areas of concern.

## An Unnatural Bill

Maria Eagle and the co-sponsors of her Bill, Respect and the RSPCA, seemed to stick to much the same menu of assumptions about this husbandry. The government is likely to use much the same rhetoric. It is a menu which seeks to make a case that mink farming is uniquely bad. The case is built up by first asserting that the mink is a wild animal, and a solitary predator at that. The argument is that in its 70 or so generations of captivity the mink could not have changed in evolutionary terms sufficiently for it to have adapted to being caged in close proximity to its fellows.

This case continues by stressing that the mink lives in relatively barren, small cages and asserting that these cannot fully satisfy its basic needs, now identified in welfare thinking as the Five Freedoms (Webster, 1994). In fact, mink are well fed, grow well, reproduce well and have, of course, spectacular coats. It is the unnaturalness of their lives which alone seriously detains us. In particular, it is claimed that mink might benefit from more space, more amusements, and from more (or less) society. Above all, it is claimed that since mink are aquatic animals, they should have access to water for bathing, showering or even swimming.

Denial of some of these amenities is supposed to lead to stress which takes the form of fur-chewing, self-mutilation, tail-sucking and the constantly-repeated rushing about, twirling, head-spinning and other repeated, energetic behaviour patterns which are called stereotypies and which are seen in different forms in elephants and bears and many other animals in confined and deprived situations (Budiansky, 1994).

And then, finally, it is claimed, the animals receive a ghastly death by gassing (though lethal injection is also allowed). We will look at all these allegations closely, and find them wanting.

But before we start examining these propositions in some detail, it is important to re-emphasise that they all involve large amounts of theory and assumption. As we discuss them, it is worth remembering that a visit to a mink farm shows animals which seem rather more alert and lively than the average and very familiar domestic rabbit. It also shows animals which never live more than six months unless to become engaged in the breeding activity which we have every evidence to suppose is a chief joy in the lives of all animals.

## Are Farmed Mink Wild Animals?

Are mink domesticated? Or, to put the issue a little differently, are they wild? Does the fact that that they are predators make any difference to either of these issues? It is clear that farmed mink are not domesticated animals in the sense that they are not normally much like the domestic animals we have at home. They are not tame. One mink farmer told me that he had a neighbour who likes him to give her young mink because she brings them up as house animals. I have also heard researchers say that this is a very unlikely event, and that mink will always be unreliable in close proximity to humans. But in any case, the case of an individual mink which was specially domesticated, or tamed, does not take one very far. The mink on a farm are not handled by humans every day, and are never petted by humans. They are curious about humans, but grow impatient and even anxious if humans hang about longer than they are used to.

In this sense, mink are indeed not domesticated. But then, in this sense, neither is the pig or cow or chicken, and few people throw the accusation at the herdsman or the poultryman that he is abusing an animal which is not domesticated. Indeed, a Danish researcher has pointed out to me that in contrast to other farm animals the mink has precisely the advantage of not having been subject to enormous genetic changes. That is, it has not been aggressively bred for fast or lean growth. The pig, cow and chicken have all suffered from aspects of this sort of breeding, and the pig and chicken have been - thankfully - the subject of what might be called de-breeding in recent years. It has often been argued that the cow is 'over-engineered' for stupendous lactation (Webster, 1994).

The mink has been bred almost exclusively with an eye to the convenience of both the farmer and the animal. Are we to believe that it is a uniquely lucky farmed animal: sufficiently bred away from wildness to be well-adapted to its circumstances, but not so over-engineered that its productivity has brought new problems? Why not might this be true? It is true that there are welfare issues surrounding selective breeding for certain types of coat: but it would be easier and sounder to outlaw or reform these rare practices within the husbandry than to ban the husbandry outright.

If the mink has suffered less than some animals at the hands of breeders, has it been changed enough to make it a good candidate for captivity? The average male farmed mink is twice the size of his wild counterpart, but he is not grossly fat, nor has he grown so fast that his legs have difficulty supporting him (the fate, until recently, of at least some chickens). The female mink has more living young than is normal under the harsh conditions of the wild, but surviving young are a useful indicator of a species' well-being, and can be thought so in this case. She certainly does not have to produce abnormal quantities of milk, as the cow does, nor breed more frequently than is 'natural' as does the sow.

It is supposed by the campaigners against fur farming that the mink is wild, and remains wild in spite of their generations of breeding. What does this mean? The cat, to take a rather similar example, is the most domesticated animal we know, and yet it remains in important respects wild. Most cats, however domesticated and docile, are capable hunters. Many cats have left their captivity or domestication and become competent feral animals, living in the wild. So the undoubted truth that some escaped mink set up in the wild with apparent success must imply that they are at least wild in the sense that the domestic cat is. But by the same token, the mink may not be any more wild than the domestic cat, either.

To keep a cat in a cage would be supposed by many to abuse its nature. We would somehow feel that it is very different from keeping a rabbit or a hen in a cage. But actually, whatever we think about the prospect of moving our adult pet cat and making it live the rest of its life alone in a cage is not to be compared with keeping a mink in a cage. It is not even to be compared with keeping caged a cat bred after generations of caged captivity. It is 70 generations since mink were removed from their wild lives and, doubtless rudely, shoved into cages. We can reasonably assume that something has happened to them since.

We do not have to believe that mink have become domestic animals (as though they were pets), nor that they have given up all the characteristics of being wild (any more than if they were urban flat-dwelling cats). Even so, they may be very different from their wild cousins.

Seventy generations of mink breeding are claimed by some British scientists to be too short a time to produce evolutionary changes by natural selection. But natural selection is not what is at work here. Very intensive selective breeding is what has taken place. Mink farmers have required animals which produced many fit young, grew good hair, and did not fight or self-mutilate. Those animals which rebelled against captivity by not reproducing naturally were lost to the gene pool, naturally. Those that had other undesirable traits were deliberately excluded from it.

It is said that the first few generations see the most genetic changes in animals when they are bred in captivity (See Appendix 1). So seventy or more years ago, there may have been a good deal of suffering before the strains of animals which could not thrive in captivity were bred out. Even since then there might have been a good deal of suffering if - as has not been demonstrated - fur farmers were indifferent to the stress and misery of their animals, but were yet able to get good commercial results from them.

To reinforce a sense that we can be fairly relaxed about the well-being of mink on farms, we can take the visual evidence of watching them and wondering how breeding might have produced such an effect. But there is also good scientific insight that all animals bred for domestication have smaller brains, which perhaps accounts for the relative docility we can see in them (See Appendix 1).

This modern strand of arguments sits well with others that suggest that animals subject to captive breeding will often maintain into adulthood features which more normally belong to the young of their species (Budiansky, 1994). These characteristics include curiosity, trustingness, and a delight in affection. These characteristics are brought about, in the wild or in captivity, by a propensity to breed from animals before they are fully adult. It happens in the wild when species colonise fresh territory. Fearless and curious animals, which will mostly be young, breed most successfully in new circumstances and have the advantage of a relatively unexplored ecological niche in which to do it. In domestication, this sort of process is hurried along and intensified by selection by the farmer's breeding programme, which seeks the same qualities and enjoys the third feature of youthful animals (less useful in nature), an affectionate, or at least amenable, nature.

Called neoteny, this phenomenon is explored most comprehensively in Stephen Budiansky's *Covenant of the Wild: Why Animals Choose Domestication* (Budiansky, 1994). He argues that it applies to humans, too: all domesticated species have what might be called juvenile traits. These include a

50

responsiveness to certain facial features: large eyes, for instance. Thus, it is argued, adult humans are very susceptible to the aesthetic appeal of young animals, and those animals which remain wide-eyed in adulthood. This helps explain the hopelessly ingrained anthropomorphism of humans. It is not that we are thoughtful about them, or considerate of them, and that we consider the care which we owe animals. No, we are moved by them as by our own young. We are, in the truest sense of the word, sentimental about them.

Professor Harris has told me that one of the reasons he is suspicious that mink might be called domesticated is that animals so bred lose their ability to develop good fur.[10] I have never seen evidence for that view, and it flies in the face of what we know about selective breeding. This suggests, rather, that animals may quite quickly become well-adapted, innately and literally, to captivity, whilst self-evidently keeping good fur-growing qualities.

## Are Captive Mink 'Happy'?

We are necessarily a little at sea when we seek to understand whether an animal is 'happy' about its lot, and even more so when we consider what might be done to make it more happy or less miserable.

The most respectable assumption is that no one measure is likely to be enough. We certainly cannot go by appearances alone, or - which is often the same sort of approach - by analogy to human wants. The most famous example of where this can go astray was in work which assumed that chickens in battery cages would be bound to prefer to have something more substantial than wire under their claws. It was not until Marian Dawkins of Oxford University started to inquire of chickens what they wanted, or rather, what they preferred, that we developed techniques for interrogating animals. The results were often counter-intuitive (Dawkins, 1993).

---

[10] Telephone conversation, 1999.

This sort of work is relevant, but conclusions from it can be pushed too far. Some of the best recent work on mink farming has, like Marian Dawkins', come from the department of zoology at Oxford University. One piece of research 'asked' mink whether they would work hard in order to have access to swimming water. It turned out that they would work quite hard for it -- harder than they would for a larger cage, for instance (Mason, 1999). Some Danish researchers say that it has not been demonstrated that mink for long go on relishing the novelty of bathing water (Hansen, 1995; Skovgaard, Jeppesen, and Hansen, 1997). The English researchers as strongly assert that they have demonstrated that they do persist in the new taste.

Either way, this work does not by any means prove that mink suffer when they do not have bathing water. We know nothing about the feelings of mink who have never known water, nor what they feel once they are used to the fact that whilst it was once available it no longer is.

This leaves us in a peculiar position. We have every reason to suppose that mink are quite like their wild cousins and at the same time quite unlike them. Given a chance, they seem to like swimming. Does it represent a denial, then, that the vast majority of mink never have a swim?

We can never ask a mink about these matters. Animals cannot tell us whether they have a definite or even a vague longing for things they do not currently have or have never had. We certainly cannot ask a mink what its perception of its unmet needs might be. It cannot itemise or prioritise its unmet needs for us. It cannot say that it has vague ideas of discontent, or precise ones. It may or may not have a notion of unmet need, or may or may not have discontents to which it could put no name, nor imagine any particular cure.

Mink might quite like swimming or bathing, or even like them very much, when they have them, just as humans might like the idea of holidays in the Seychelles. But consider the implications of this analogy. Most people long for a holiday in the Seychelles long before they actually enjoy one. Most people for all of history have had a long list of desirable things which they saw all about them but they could never have. Once you were on a holiday in the Seychelles, and were enjoying it, you would be very upset if it was suddenly truncated. You might be angry if you were told that though an anticipated holiday in the Seychelles had been promised, it was now to be denied you.

But we ought to understand that most people never have a holiday in the Seychelles; a holiday in the Seychelles is no one's birthright; people might not as much enjoy a holiday in the Seychelles as they expect to; one might work hard for a holiday in the Seychelles much more for the fact of putting one's feet up than because one wanted, especially, to put one's feet up in the Seychelles; someone who had loved a holiday in the Seychelles but knew he could never have another might well be regarded as better off than someone who had never known a holiday in the Seychelles at all; even people who long for a holiday in the Seychelles might very quickly concede that there are far more important things in life. Above all, no-one has ever claimed that, for all its being very pleasurable, people can expect a holiday in the Seychelles, still less should such an exotic holiday be listed as a prime need for people.

Similar questions fairly arise about mink and their willingness to work for bathing water. We cannot ask them for their answers to the questions, but our own answers to analogous ones indicate that merely because an animal will work for things does not mean that they are necessary or even important.

One way of looking at this issue is to suppose, as some recent work suggests, that animals have innate needs. Roger Scruton, for instance, believes that horses have an innate need to run with the herd, even if they have never done so.[11] This language suggests that animals may have needs which are not translated into wants: but this seems a little like suggesting that a need can be a sort of unexpressed want. What would it mean to want something without knowing it or feeling it? Chickens go through the motions of dust-bathing, whether or not they have dust available. Is this a need? Does this mean they suffer if they never actually dust-bathe? One

---

[11] Private note, but see Scruton, 1996

might make a case, but not prove it, that hens might more miss dust-bathing than mink miss swimming. Mink do not make the motions of swimming and bathing in the absence of the sort of water in which they might swim and bathe. They do not seem hard-wired to swim in the way that hens are hard-wired to dust-bathe.

Still, knowing that mink do swim in the wild remains troubling. Even the possibility that they may dislike swimming in the wild and do it only because they need to will not give us much comfort. We are trying to make them happy in captivity, and in captivity we have good evidence that they like swimming, given the chance. They may do it with quite different emotions than they swim in the wild. We simply do not know. Still, we would need decent evidence that mink do not miss swimming and do not need swimming for their welfare, if we wanted to continue to allow farmers not to provide swimming water.

Can we demonstrate that mink are well off in spite of lacking facilities which it appears likely they would enjoy if they had them? This is where we need to look at other welfare indicators from amongst the bundle of parameters by which we might judge mink, or any, animal welfare.

The most obvious one would be to look for signs of stress or discontent in mink farms. There is a quite large literature about stereotypies, which are repeated, abnormal behaviour patterns (Budiansky, 1994; Hansen, 1995; CUAWIC). They are often seen in captive animals. Elephants swing their trunks and sway their bodies, often in unison with their companions, when bored in their lines at circuses. Bears and other animals pace repeatedly along the same, sometimes apparently irrational track, in zoos. These repeated activities are often signs of boredom. In more frenzied form, they are taken to be signs of stress and anxiety.

This behaviour in animals has always been recognised as a sign of their discontent. Cardinal Newman, for instance, used it as a paradigm of the human soul's unhappiness (in his Dream of Gerontius, set to fabulous music by Edward Elgar:

It is the restless panting of their beings:

Like beasts of prey, who, caged within their bars,
In a deep hideous purring have their life,
And an incessant pacing to and fro.

In their version these discontented mink are said to fight, chew their own tails and mutilate themselves: these activities are said by protesters to be common.

Mink certainly have been found to perform stereotypies and all the rest on farms. There are references in research papers to mink doing so for up to half their waking hours. But the fact that some references get stuck into the literature of this behaviour having been seen is no more interesting than, for instance, a selective fact about a celebrity getting stuck in the cuttings file of a news agency. Before the cutting is of value in assessing the celebrity's current style of life, one would first of all need to know whether the cutting was ever or importantly true, and secondly whether it continued to be true. What is more, thirdly, the behaviour of one celebrity might not be a very good indicator of the behaviour of all celebrities.

Contrary to what is said by the campaigners and what is relied upon by the Cambridge survey of research papers, there is rather little evidence that nowadays mink must or even often do have behavioural oddities on mink farms, and relying on a very few rather old papers does not help people grasp the fact.

Continental researchers who might be supposed to know about it insist that stereotypies are not all that common on mink farms. They also suggest that these aberrancies are not the best evidence of animal welfare. They come to this conclusion by drawing on evidence that animals which are in other ways showing signs of good welfare are more, rather than less prone, to show stereotypies.

This is evidence which bites both ways. If animals displaying stereotypies are coping rather well, does this imply that animals which do not stereotype may actually be suffering rather more, but - so to speak - in silence? Now that stereotypies are rare, does this imply that the suffering of which they are visible sign has been driven, so to speak, underground?

55

How might we give an animal which shows no outward signs of suffering the benefit of the doubt? How might we pursue the issue of its well-being beyond its glossy coat, its appetite, the large number of its healthy progeny, its apparent lively but relaxed behaviour? There is, mercifully, another piece of welfare armoury which can be deployed. It is, like any of the others, not much use by itself, and it throws up conflicting messages. But it must surely be seen as contributing to a picture of tolerable welfare.

Work in Denmark assesses the levels of various hormones to be found in the urine of mink in different situations. Put simply, this sort of work, widespread in animal and human physiological studies, distinguishes between an animal's periodically producing stress hormones in response to challenges it deems exciting or frightening, and its having - very differently - constantly to produce them because its entire life is one of stress and frustration. The production of stress hormones in the short-term can be taken to be a good or a bad thing according to whether one thinks that an animal has been subjected, say, to sudden and fearful events, or to the expectation of pleasurable ones. An animal anticipating unpleasantness will produce stress hormones, but these will also be an indication, for instance, that the animal expects shortly to have intercourse or food. The chemical signs of excitement do not distinguish between these very different stimuli.

In either case the animal is readying itself for activity, whether fighting, fleeing, feeding or fornicating. If challenges continue for too long, too continuously, the animal's 'base' level of hormones becomes high. It moves from registering occasional bursts of excited preparedness to maintaining constant high levels of production of hormones in a way which becomes a drain on its metabolic resources.

We can readily see why this might be so. These 'readiness' responses signal and trigger a diversion of resources - energy, blood - away from functions such as digestion, the immune system, reproduction. An animal cannot indefinitely repair these systems whilst diverting energy to the permanent maintenance of a system designed for period use.

The Danish researches into these hormone levels suggest that healthy mink on well-run farms display satisfactory levels of intermittent hormone production and equally satisfactory levels of background hormone. In other words, by the indicator of hormone production farmed mink seem to be in satisfactory metabolic condition.

One other indicator is prayed in aid of the idea that mink routinely suffer. Some research suggests that they suffer high levels of stomach ulcers, a classic indicator of routine excesses of stress. But actually, one specialist Danish researcher stresses that stomach ulcers are not very common in mink, and where they do occur, do so at rather low levels. It is not even clear that stomach ulcers are a clear indicator of stress: they are as likely to be an indicator of bacterial infection. [12] (Harri, et al, 1995).

We can see now how the welfare of mink does not conform at all well to the protesters' ideas of it. We can look at the ordinary person's perception of mink on farms; at some ideas about ethology; at the metabolic status of the animals, and wherever we go we find evidence that it makes decent sense to say that the animals appear to be quite well off. There is no overwhelming evidence from most of the parameters that might dismay us. A worrying question remains: is the element of doubt sufficient to make us want to improve the animals' welfare?

## Mink Welfare Reform

Suppose we were not content with the welfare of mink, and wanted to do something about it. Where would we begin? There is the laborious process to discuss improvement in mink welfare at

---

[12] Jan Elnif, associate professor of fur animal science, department of animal science and health, royal veterinary and agricultural university, Denmark, says: 'The ulcer frequency is very low in Danish farmed mink. It is not a main disorder that gives us any reason for concern. I know that it is possible to provoke ulcers experimentally. The whole point of view on ulcers has been shifting quite a lot, as people have discovered that there are bacterial factors behind ulcers, and they can often be cured by eliminating certain bacteria'.

European Union and Council of Europe levels, and the latter has produced guidelines which broadly enshrine the best of the existing Danish practices. One of the prime requirements mink appear to 'request' in behavioural tests is a nesting box. This has now been an absolute minimum requirement on mink farms for years, and no one disputes its value. It might seem a kind idea to give mink more space, and new Council of Europe guidelines enshrine this idea. Research suggests that actually mink place only a medium priority on this, but it is a move which satisfies human prejudices and may be useful to the mink, too.

One of the problems in mink welfare is to know what sort of social lives the animals might benefit from. It is interesting that the protesters often draw attention to the fact that the mink is solitary in the wild. From this it is commonly deduced that the proximity of one caged mink to another is offensive to them. It is true that mink seem happiest if they cannot even see their neighbours at certain times of the year, but it is equally true that they benefit from visual contact at other times (CUAWIC, no date).

There is good evidence that young mink do best if they are allowed to stay with their mother for some time, and indeed for roughly the period they would have with her in the wild (CUAWIC, Hansen, 1995). It is not easy to be sure what is the ideal weaning period: it might not match the period the mother tolerates her young around the nest in the wild before she boots them out to fend for themselves. In the wild, there may be a good deal of unpleasantness in that period, and there is evidence that early weaning benefits the mother's welfare (CUAWIC, no date).

Modern mink farmers tend to allow about 7 or 8 weeks before weaning the young, and it is suggested that this should be extended to about 11 weeks, a practice which has been shown to reduce tail-biting in the young. I any case, farmers then do something that absolutely does not happen in the wild, and which the protesters complain about, but which seems to be a major contributor to the well-being of the young.

At about the time when young mink would be hunting and establishing themselves as solitary animals, farmed mink are put in sibling pairs. It may well be that these young then establish a pecking order, but if so there is no sign of aggressiveness or bullying. Indeed, the mink seem to spend a good deal of time curled up together. Prolonged sibling companionship, is perhaps a sign of what can be achieved with animals who are brought up in particular behaviour patterns when very young. But, like the value of delayed weaning, it also fits with general research that suggests that very young animals go on to flourish if they have what might as well be called emotional support in their earliest days and weeks (Sapolsky, 1994). What is more it fits with ideas we gather from neoteny about domesticated animals being particularly hungry for warmth, attention and companionship (Budiansky, 1994).

The majority of farmed mink, then, are born and then go on to have particularly warm and close relations with various close family members for the few months they live until they are slaughtered.

A proportion of young mink are selected to go on to have two, three, four or even more years as breeding mothers, which have a solitary life punctuated by rearing young for the spring and summer months. The far less numerous breeding males have the same number of years with a yet more solitary life which is only interrupted during a period as studs for a month every year. Both these adult females and males seem to thrive, but there is legitimate discussion about what could plausibly be done to improve their lot.

One possibility is to take the same amount of space as is occupied by solitary cages and to see if social groups might be arranged to provide more interest to the breeding females and males. So far, research indicates that some approaches to group housing might be commercially possible and beneficial in welfare terms, but on neither count is it overwhelming (Spruijt, 1996).

Interestingly, one avenue that might prove profitable draws on the idea that the problem for mink in captivity may not be that they suffer so much as that they might be bored. They may need more of the right kind of stress. Mink are certainly very interested in their food: most stereotypy behaviour appears to have taken place when mink had long waits for it and they become excited before feeding time on the best regulated farms. (The breeding females and males get very agitated, too, in the run-up to breeding: rather as humans do.) This behaviour may not be deserved to have been called stereotypy at all: any domestic cat gets very excited, and paces up and down, when it senses the availability of food.

Canny management of feed times has hugely contributed to reducing stereotypies (Budiansky, 1994; Wiepkema, 1994). It may be that a useful approach to mink welfare will be not the provision of more facilities of the kind which might seem obviously comfortable, but the provision of more work and more challenges in their lives. It might be that working harder for food, or displaying more ingenuity before getting it, might produce more of the 'good' kind of stress and stave off the bad kind of stress which might be supposed to, but cannot be seen to, have arisen from boredom.

It makes sense to continue to put a certain amount of effort into researching improvements in mink welfare. These efforts should not be seen as exceptionally necessary to . redeem an exceptionally cruel practice: they should be seen in the context of the continuing need to see what can reasonably be done to improve the lot of all the animals we keep for our convenience and pleasure.

We need to continue to stress that mink do not have atrocious lives, and also to suggest that they face up to the way these and other animals die. Mink are, as the protesters never fail to point out, gassed.[13] Professor Harris went so far on West Eye View as to equate this gassing with what happened to the Jews in the holocaust.

---

[13] EU and UK welfare regulations allow three methods for slaughtering farmed mink – by **lethal injection** of a drug with anaesthetic properties, or **inhalation methods** using carbon monoxide or carbon dioxide. Farmers tend to believe that lethal injection is the most distressing of the three for animals. In the UK farmers favour $CO_2$ while in Holland carbon monoxide is preferred.

It happens that gassing a creature with carbon monoxide is one of the least traumatic ways to kill it and that this is so much the case that it has seemed a bad idea to have carbon monoxide in common use. Suicides have always favoured it. The trade has been constrained to use carbon dioxide instead. Now it is true, as research has indicated of mink, that given the choice creatures will not voluntarily inhale carbon dioxide (Cooper & Mason, 1998). But CO2, which is used on mink farms produces unconsciousness in a very few seconds, and death in about half a minute. It does not matter how true it is that gassing was used in a great human tragedy, nor that researchers can show that given a choice, mink will shy away from the stuff. What matters is that every year mink farmers walk quietly down their rows of cages and quietly pick up one animal after another and place it firmly into a box within which the mink has no choice but quickly and quietly to inhale what is at first an anaesthetic and then a killer.

It is not given to any other farm animal to have so quick and quiet a dispatch. The mink does not suffer the surprise and shock of suddenly being transported many miles to a slaughter house. It has instead a death which would be the envy of any of us were it not for our entirely reasonable expectation that the timing of our death should not be in the hands of people who are thinking of their convenience rather than ours. The mink, like other animals, has no such awareness of impending death.

We need to touch briefly on the issue of fox farming, though none of that is done in the UK. This is a practice mostly carried out in the northern Scandinavian countries, and it raises many of the issues which apply to mink. There are significant differences, though. The literature on these animals is much more slight, but leads to a conclusion which is at first rather worrying.

Foxes seem to have a rather complicated social life: it is solitary and sociable by turns, and in rather complicated ways (CUAWIC, no date). The upshot seems to be that foxes thrive best if it is understood that they seem to have a virtually inalienable sense of social status, and need to be kept in such a way that a dominant animal is not placed too near a very subordinate one, even if they are in separate cages.

There is good evidence that foxes respond well to quite aggressive social contact with humans (CUAWIC, no date). Rough but affectionate handling when young seems to have the effect of habituating them to contact with humans, and makes their life on farms pleasanter than if they are left alone, and in a state of natural dread of their keepers. These are essentially tameable animals, and in that sense they are very different from mink. They may be brought far more easily and obviously positively to like their human captors. Again, experiments are taking place which give foxes a far more social life than they normally have in their solitary cages: it may turn out that these work well.

The literature and discussions with researchers tends to suggest that fox-keeping can be and often is done well.

## Trapped Animals

The fur trade has a slightly easier job when it comes to defending fur-trapping. After all, the lives the animals live in the wild, however awful, are not its business. It has only to take account of the deaths of the animals it traps.

The archetypal image of the fur trade comes from the north American outback where white or indigenous trappers work traplines many miles from civilisation. The modern reality has changed a little. Trappers tend to be able to commute to their lines more easily, and to move around them on motorised snowmobiles rather than with dog sleds.

Trappers have changed much. The white trapper will often be the owner of a fishing concession and a tourist business, with trapping a partial support to see him through the winter. The indigenous trapper will often be an Indian, or further north, an Inuit. But nowadays he (or she, many of the best hunters are women) will usually be an individual who is disinclined to spend his or her life entirely dependent on welfare, which is the dominant experience of the vast majority of non-whites who stay in their homelands.

It happens that the whites are on average more dedicated and efficient trappers than the non-whites (known in Canada as aboriginals, or First Nation peoples), so they contribute disproportionately to the harvest of fur-bearing animals.

There have been repeated attempts to defend the north American fur-trade as a bolster to the dignity and economy of the indigenous peoples, and that is fair enough so far as it goes. However, it is worth remembering that far more fur comes from the fur-farms in the region than from traplines and even in the case of the latter, more from whites than from aboriginals.

Even so, the fundamental appeal of trapped fur over farmed fur ought to be that the animals killed are wild; and the men and women who take them are brave and hardy; and the activity takes place in country of austere, wild beauty.

In animal welfare terms, the prime defence of fur trapping ought to be that it rather reduces animal suffering in the wild than increases it. The human dimension is moving, but it would hardly by itself legitimise animal suffering, were that to be much increased by human activity. Oddly enough, though, trapped animals in the wild almost always have less painful and prolonged deaths than are accorded to their fellows which die naturally.

This counter-intuitive fact is simply explained. Left to themselves, wild fur-bearing animals die from accident, disease or decrepitude, all of which finally mean they can no longer hunt, so they go on to freeze or starve. It is no use thinking about trapping as though the fate of animals would otherwise be a Disney romance. Wild animals live in a desperately hard environment and with a natural fate of appalling brutality. Nature is neither moral nor kind. The men and women who go trapping understand this and are able to see, what the rest of us seldom can, that their work needs only to stand comparison, not with a romance of the wild, but its reality.

The majority of trapped animals are small enough to be caught in traps which are designed to kill their victim very nearly instantaneously. The efficiency of these traps is demonstrated in research programmes, especially in Canada, where methods are tested for reliability. The vast majority of animals taken in these traps are killed within seconds, or at most a few minutes (Appendix 2). There must be failures and mistakes, and these doubtless cause suffering. Researchers and knowledgeable trappers claim these accidental victims are few, and the suffering they cause needs to be set in the context of the common and regular possibility of accidents occurring in the wild anyway.

Trapping is controlled so that only abundant species are trapped, and only trapped when they are abundant and not breeding. Fur-bearers are killed in their full winter coat, when their young, if any, can fend for themselves.

Only the large animals are trapped in devices which are designed to hold them until the hunter returns to dispatch them. The majority of such animals - say wolf, fox and lynx - are taken using the leghold trap. It is a standard claim by protesters that animals caught in these traps are mutilated by the action of the jaws and then suffer as they struggle to release themselves.

There is indeed apparently powerful video and photographic evidence of animals struggling in leghold traps. However, that may be no more than evidence that some at least of the suffering endured by trapped animals occurs when humans approach them whilst the animals cannot flee.

The clearest evidence that leghold traps do not conform to the protesters' stereotypes is their use in situations where conservation managers want to move individuals or whole packs of wolf or fox from near towns. Here, the leghold trap is used because it is capable of holding the animal unharmed for later release. Trap researchers insist that there is good evidence that animals caught in leghold traps most usually lie quietly when held, and especially if the trap is placed so that the animal can get itself into a sheltered place where it will be undisturbed. The only kind of leghold trap now permitted in north America is designed to hold but not to tear or damage an animal's leg: after a great deal of persuasion and doubt I once allowed one to be snapped onto my hand without feeling pain.

The leghold is commonly used to trap beaver: in this case, the animal is held underwater, and it seems obvious that it will drown. Actually, beaver trapped underwater have a quieter death than might be supposed. Because they hold their breath, they in effect die from carbon dioxide poisoning within three or four minutes of being trapped. They do not drown at all; they asphyxiate (Appendix 2).

Obviously, there is a profound distinction between a trap designed to kill outright and one designed to hold an animal alive, and it is hardly surprising that there have been many proposals to outlaw the leghold: these have now reached the point where the major players (as concerned consumers, or producers: the EU, US, Canada and Russia) have agreed to submit evidence to a Council of Europe forum about the humaneness of any leghold or other trap they plan to use, or accept a ban at least on the sale of fur animals caught in prohibited traps.

In the meantime, it is useful to note that the majority of animals trapped in legholds meet this fate for conservation reasons. The animals suffer in some degree, but not because of the fur trade. The pity of it is that, having suffered in some degree, the full value to humans of the by-product - their fur - is not utilised. The authorities in Louisiana, for instance, pay for huge numbers of nutria (called coypu in Europe) to be trapped: a better acceptance of the practice and a more vigorous fur trade would merely ensure the costs of the operation were met by consumers rather than taxpayers, whilst giving people the pleasure of wearing fur (Appendix 3). In the Netherlands, hundreds of thousands of coypu are trapped every year to preserve the dyke system: but the sale of the fur is banned, so it is wasted.

The public sometimes has a lingering expectation that the wild animals it loves are at risk from the fur trade. Actually most trapping is done for conservation or species management reasons. There is a persistent misunderstanding that the fur trade uses or endangers rare species. The facts are that the fur trade is very highly visible and that the trapped furs it can use have for at least two decades been regulated under CITES regulations designed to prevent trade in endangered species.[14] There is good evidence that there are more of most of the trapped species than there were several hundred years ago.

---

[14] The British Fur Trade Association adds: 'International Fur Trade Federation statistics show that 90% of all animals trapped in the wild each year are not trapped directly for fur but for other purposes such as wildlife conservation, pest control, etc. mostly in Russia, the EU & North America. The image of a fur trade responsible for trapping animals is also false. For example in the EU hundreds of thousands of muskrats are trapped every year to halt damage to dykes in Germany and Holland, but the skins are not used. In the US, the skins from such programmes are utilised by the fur trade. Essentially wild fur such as beaver, muskrat & opossum is a by-product of wildlife management. For example in New Zealand, the World Wide Fund for Nature (WWF) actively promotes possum fur because the animal is such a pest – more than 70 million at last count – and is harming the native forests, etc. The sale of skins helps towards the cost of the management programmes. The International Agreements on Humane Trapping Standards were signed up to in 1997 by Russia, EU, USA & Canada.'

# 3. The Authorities

Fur-wearing is deeply offensive to a small minority of the public. These people must be allowed to protest however wrong or silly many of their arguments and views are.

Some of the protest takes place every Saturday outside the two furriers in the West End, and during the week outside the remaining furrier in Knightsbridge. Sometimes this protest is dignified. In these moments, it has something of the character of bearing silent witness. But more often, it is noisy and sometimes it is directed full-on, face-to-face at any customers daring to run the gauntlet. The shouted slogans tend to include: 'Fur trade, death trade', and anyone working in the shops or using them will be routinely called a murderer, scum, and worse.

At least this protest is happening in roughly the right place: in public. However, some of the more committed protesters pride themselves on getting the home addresses of anyone - customer or staff - associated with the trade. At home, such people will often get oh-so polite letters reminding them of their moral duty to animals and inviting them to reconsider their work or purchases. To receive such mail is of course very frightening. The letters are mild enough, but they clearly signal, what the protesters will sometimes whisper to people they know are associated with the trade: 'we know where you live'. We know what that means when we hear in a gangster movie and we know what it means when George Robertson, the defence secretary, uses it in the House of Commons of Slobodan Milosovic of Yugoslavia. The letters addressed to employees' homes could all perfectly easily, and more appropriately one might think, be directed to the individuals at work: but they are written to people at home, and surely for a purpose.

This behaviour is meant to be menacing, and is. Furriers have on occasion received letter bombs at home, though not recently. Small chanting crowds, damaged cars and daubed signs are the more normal recent currency. The threat of worse, and the memory of worse, keeps the furriers under the hammer.

Oddly, the animal rights protesters outside retailers are not above using racial abuse to any black person they know to be associated with the fur trade. Some protesters draw their finger across their throat when looking at customers or staff. Some of these signs are less ambivalent than others.

Should right-minded people give protest the benefit of the doubt when this sort of thing goes on, or masked groups visit fur farmers and fur merchants at home and daub their houses with slogans, slash their car tyres, leaflet their neighbours suggesting that the target is a paedophile?

What are we to make of the disclaimers of visible groups like Respect that the shadowy groups are nothing to do with them? The routine response by public spokesmen tends to be something like, 'We do not do this sort of thing ourselves, and cannot condone it, but we do not condemn it either, and we understand how people who feel strongly about animals may well in their passion behave in this way towards people who make animals suffer'. Even the Animal Liberation Front does not claim itself to be murderous, but does operate what one newspaper called a 'Sinn Fein-IRA relationship' with the harder types of the 'Animal Rights Militia', whose death threats against vivisectionists the ALF relays (*Sunday Times*, 1998a).

Surely the 'more respectable' are made less so when the tone of their disavowal is so feeble? Should we not treat their moral case about animals with scepticism when the moral quality of their human behaviour is so flawed? It would be one thing to reach for protest of any sort in a situation where debate was stifled and legislation patently undemocratic, but those of us who inhabit a media world and a democracy should surely wonder when we watch confrontational behaviour and worse from campaigners.

There is of course a long tradition of radical dissent, and religious dissent, and it has always perturbed onlookers to decide whether it was the fanaticism or the idealism of the extremist which most struck them. In the 17th century Antinomianism was identified as the condition of believing that one's religious cause put one above the law (Hill, 1975). More recently, the word has been used to suggest the kind of extreme Bohemianism which the early 19th century Romantics adopted as an almost deliberate and very secular affront to society (Johnson, 1991). Given so responsive and permissive a society as ours, modern extreme protest might reasonably be taken to be something volunteered for and enjoyed, rather than something people are constrained to undertake if they are to make any progress at all. The difficulty now is to understand how seriously to take the protest: should we take it at the protesters' own estimation, or are we free - obliged, even - to put their passion on one side and look merely at their case? We are brought up to believe that martyrdom has an honourable tradition, but what are we to make of a Barry Horne, who is serving an 18 year sentence for a two year fire-bombing campaign, and who in December 1998 threatened to starve himself to death unless the government set up a royal commission on animal experimentation? Was he a martyr or a blackmailer? Luckily, one might say, most of us did not have to make a judgement: the government declared itself not open to blackmail and Horne resumed his vegan diet, though with what were reported to be irreversible health effects from his action (*Sunday Telegraph*, 1998a). Barry Horne was said by one of his acquaintances to be obsessive: 'He has no social life to speak of, his only passion is animals'. But this is not the whole picture: an activist who left the ALF told one newspaper that, 'The whole time I was with them, we never actually discussed animals. They are not really animal lovers... They are anarchists who view the use of animals as a political conspiracy and human cruelty. Some of them even told me they do not even like animals. They use the argument that you do not have to like black people to want to liberate them. It is a mindset which allows you to bomb people with immunity (sic)' (*Sunday Telegraph*, 1998b). Modern protest can turn into terrorism 'inspired by single issues, such as environmental degradation, animal rights, or abortion', according to the International Institute of Strategic Studies (*The Times*, 1999c).

Part of the difficulty is that whilst it is clear that almost all the active protesters against fur indulge in some unpleasant behaviour or worse, it is very hard to prove that many of these visible protesters are the same people as turn up in balaclavas at the homes of furriers, fur-farmers, and people engaged in other pariah-status animal trades.

The treatment of those involved in animal experimentation, no matter how innocent, is a case in point. In the summer of 1999, after two years of intense campaigning and high profile demonstrations, various groups, including Save the Hillgrove Cats succeeded in forcing Christopher Brown to give up his cat farming business in Oxfordshire. In the period Thames Valley Police spent £3 million protecting the farm, at least 350 have been arrested and 21 jailed for public order offences. Mr Brown's family had been firebombed, his house burnt, the windows broken on many occasions, the family's cars vandalised. Finally, in June 1999, the 62 year old farmer's wife was attacked and shackled to a fence whilst walking the family dog. She was released after ten minutes. It should be enough to say that the farm was licensed by the Home Office, that it did no experimentation, that the cats from it were mostly used for veterinary research, and that most suffered in the whole of their lives no more than any cat undergoing vaccination (*Daily Telegraph*, 1999d; Independent, 1999). The target of complaint should always have been the Home Office and Parliament, and the manner always strictly open and peaceable. Instead, there is hardly any coverage of the merits of the case for experimentation, and those, such as Professor Colin Blakemore, who are knowledgeable enough to make the case in favour must run the risk of even more intense campaigning and harassment for their pains (*Sunday Telegraph*, 1998c).

A greater difficulty is to understand where to draw the line between the competing rights of fur-protesters and fur producers or fur wearers. Should the protesters' right to protest be paralleled by the right of fur-wearers to the enjoyment of their hard-earned coat? Granted that there is a clear right to protest, should there not be a parallel right to the quiet enjoyment of legal activities, such as the purchase and wearing of fur?

How is one to police such an issue, especially granted that the protesters may actively enjoy not merely being intellectually dissident but also treasure their perceived right to break the law in their higher moral cause?

The previous government introduced legislation designed to make squatting on land and massed protests more difficult. In response to the problem of men and fans stalking women and celebrities, they introduced a measure, which became the Protection From Harassment Act, 1997, which outlawed various sorts of aggressive and persistent behaviour (Lawson-Cruttenden et al). It introduced an element of criminal law into issues which had previously been a largely civil matter and it was regarded as a rather untidy piece of work. One of its effects was to make it possible for people who could prove they were receiving very unwelcome or threatening invasion of their privacy to have a no-go area declared around their person or property. This would exclude certain named or identifiable harassers. It has been used, almost by chance, by a very few people in the fur trade to have animal rights protesters excluded from the neighbourhood of their homes.

At first, during 1998, the anti-harassment legislation was also used to exclude protesters from the close vicinity of a particular furrier's shop in the West End. A legal quirk has meant that it has not been enforced recently, because the means to declare exclusion zones came into force before the means to apply the criminal law to people who broke their terms. When the latter took effect, police felt that the plaintiffs ought to go back and get a fresh exclusion zone injunction since its effect had changed. The furrier concerned has not felt that the expense was warranted or fair.

The Harassment Act has a curious effect. Its use to protect a private address seems somehow more justified than its use around a shop, which is by definition a place in the public arena. In this latter case, the police interpreted the Act to mean that protesting groups which included people covered by the exclusion order should be kept several hundred yards from the shop front, whatever the style of protest they wanted to pursue.

No one has tested what the Act might mean in its present form for such protest, but it seems on the face of it rather heavy-handed.

For the most part, the policing of protest is a matter of the police having to prove that a definite criminal act, or obstruction, or a Breach of the Peace is likely. These last two especially are very tricky areas, with new law to be interpreted, such as the Public Order Act 1986. The police and lower courts often find themselves over-ruled by higher, or European courts (*The Times*, 1999d; *The Times*, 1998c). A policeman has to believe that confrontations are such as likely to lead to violence before he can arrest someone, who may justifiably be kept away from the scene for a while, or, in more serious cases be brought before magistrates to be bound over to keep the peace in future. An alternative is for the police to claim and prove that protesters are obstructing traffic or the pavement. These are necessarily grey areas, and recent high court and House of Lords judgements have reinforced the carefulness with which police must proceed. Several major cases have found in favour of protesters, and made the police feel less secure that old understandings about where to draw these difficult lines will be supported in court. Meanwhile, the government is consulting (as of September 1999) on proposals to bring anti-terrorist measures to bear on protesters whose actions cross from the peaceful to the threatening.

In one fascinating recent case, a magistrate in the north east allowed some highly active protesters to go free after some particularly aggressive behaviour in 'an action' at a fur farm had led to arrests. He suggested that the unpopularity of fur-farmers - which he supposed rather than proved - somehow legitimised this behaviour. In June 1999, the appeal court told him to revisit the judgement. Interestingly, whilst the protesters claim that the fur trade is unpopular, the trade has its own respectable poll evidence to support the idea that much animal rights protests offends public opinion on how far protest can legitimately go.

The judgements which appear to be rewriting the rules on protest make good reading for libertarians, and maybe for those who are not under threat of protest from animal rights or other self-appointed guardians of the nation's morals. They must please writers such as George Monbiot of the Guardian who wrote:

> 'Britain is on the brink of the biggest civil rights clamp-down in recent history... Trouble-making is a costly nuisance, a drain on public resources, an impediment to the smooth functioning of government. It is also one of the only means by which our political leaders can be forced to address the concerns of the excluded, the dispossessed or, indeed, anyone who does not number among their target audience.'

Thus speaks the joined-up-writing wing of the Swampy tendency. It is thinking reflected in many of the children of the post-war middle class and affluent who are now spear-heading campaigning activism, alongside more obviously punk ne'er-do-wells such as were seen in the recent Carnival Against Capitalism (*The Times*, 1999). It is the kind of thinking which characterised the campaigning in Seattle during the opening round of World Trade Organisation negotiations in Seattle in November 1999.

It is not clear that we are making much progress in developing a way of dealing with the increasingly vociferous and active protest against various activities which were always controversial but which protesters have made confrontational. In the cases of genetically modified organisms, hunting, fur, animal experimentation and intensive animal production for the human food chain we see five activities which pit views of man's dominion over, or obligation toward, the natural world against each other. All have produced direct action groups. All have produced threats to property. Some have produced violence, or threats of violence, against people. Any might descend into serious violence. All produce a tension between the rights of wider society and those of highly committed people who oppose each other.

In the case of fur, we can see some of these interactions at their sharpest. The broad majority of the public would at the very least tolerate the wearing of fur. But this permissiveness is not unequivocal. Many such people might nonetheless feel that the protesters are perhaps more moral, by taking an interest, than the silent majority. In any case, the opponents and the proponents of fur are both very determined. The tensions between them raise moral questions, and policing questions too. The tensions between them are not such that society can easily stand aside.

It is typical of the British approach that Parliament and the police in general do try to shield the fur trade and its customers from the worst effect of protest. But they do so within quite a firm sense that their response must not be disproportionate. Some academic researchers using animals have put up with years of more or less constant threat and abuse from protesters with few penalties imposed on the latter. Furriers and fur farmers have endured more intermittent and usually less dramatic threats, but frightening ones nonetheless.

One way to resolve the tension between protesters and the trades or practices they hate is to outlaw the latter. No one has yet dared seriously to propose a law banning the wearing of fur, but the Eagle bill was of course an attempt to outlaw fur-farming. In this it mirrored the New Labour manifesto with its overt populism and a concomitant tendency to ignore the rights of minorities, amongst them the hereditary peers, landowners, hunting people, and fur farmers.

The new government came to power with a manifesto on several of these issues. Animal rights, like countryside access and reform of the House of Lords perhaps seemed like relatively easy and attractively radical measures for a government which wanted to be thought radical but was rather thoroughly conservative.

It has found fox hunting to be a more complicated political issue than it at first thought it would be. Luckily, from its point of view, the matter was pressed by a Labour backbencher, whose private member's bill to ban hunting could and did fail without much implicating the government. Now, the government has initiated an inquiry into the likely effects of a hunting ban, and can thus delay and perhaps postpone indefinitely any further legislation.

It seems that the fur farmers have proved an irresistible target. With so many promises on 'animal welfare' made, New Labour's inner councils probably felt that something bold and clear needed to be done, somewhere. In the absence of a clear welfare logic, the government needed a new language to cover a policy which was populist, but whose enactment could not be based on anything quite so obviously flawed. 'Public morality' has been invoked as a novel ruse. It is a rather shocking new principle, since it could as easily be invoked in favour of any populist cause which claimed a moral dimension, but whose moral dimension was transparently inadequate to be argued seriously.

From a purely pragmatic point of view, the issue now facing the government is fairly simple. It said in its manifesto that it would ban fur farming, and the debates on Maria Eagle's bill has allowed it to see where the main stumbling blocks are. Beyond some issues of definition, the worst problem seems to be how badly various fur-farming nations within the EU may take a unilateral ban, and, more prosaically, what would be the right level of compensation for the farmers whose activity would be banned.

In principle, fur farming nations could probably live quite easily alongside a Britain which did not allow fur to be farmed but did not outlaw the produce of nations that did. Compensation might be a bit more difficult. Several and perhaps all British fur farmers would like to get out of the business if they could do so on terms which allowed them to set up in something else or retire. The protesters make much of the dissension within the ranks of the trade on this, noting with delight that the farmers themselves are more willing to gave up than the rest of the trade is willing to see them do so. Actually, of course, the farmers do not concede the protesters' principle, but do accept pragmatically that protest has made their lives all but intolerable. If they could be compensated sufficiently, abandoning their farms becomes attractive.

But such terms were not offered to pig farmers who were made to invest in (rather dubious) animal welfare measures or get out of the trade. Indeed, objections would certainly be raised as to why a farmer should be compensated for giving up practices which have been declared unacceptable by Parliament.

An argument in favour of so compensating fur farmers goes like this. Here is a trade of which nothing exceptional can be proved or even seriously suggested. It is a trade which is allowed by all our major trading partners. It is the subject of ongoing reform measures in international forums of which Britain is a part. It is a trade rendered expensive to undertake, and also dangerous to undertake, because of the determined and illegal activities of protesters. If such capricious measures are to be taken, every other user of animals will need reassurance that their activities are seen as legitimate, and likely to be the subject of compensation arrangements. Otherwise who would dare invest in an industry which might suddenly be shut down on a protest whim, or on the grounds of 'public morality'?

It is not surprising that its practitioners are willing to get out of the trade if they can without ruining themselves, but it would be quite wrong to outlaw them as though to do so had been the result of serious investigation and thorough argumentation.

This is the heart of the problem. Proper compensation offered to fur farmers would carry the implication that the government accepted that the farmers had been the innocent victim of arbitrary parliamentary sanction which was not based on any very large or legitimate principle. And yet anyone proposing a ban on fur-farming would like to be arguing that it was just, right, obvious, and clear that the practice was not merely unpopular, but actually wrong, and more wrong than any similar practices which had not been banned. Presumably, anyone discriminated against without compensation could go before a European forum and claim that his human rights had been violated. There, the disparity of view between, say, Denmark and Britain would be rather clear.

A libertarian, free market view would probably suggest that from the farmers' point of view, it would only be fair to compensate them well for being discriminated against. And a taxpayer would then be nudged towards the view that it could hardly be right to introduce legislation so unfair that it required compensation of its victims to make it morally acceptable. The voter would probably suppose that sooner than pay compensation, Parliament should ask itself very seriously why it wanted to introduce a very selective ban on just one use of animals.

More generally, and culturally, it is a curious society which has no interest in condemning the kinds of actions which stop willing customers buying from willing sellers in a legal and policed trade committed to reform. It is an odder one still which does not notice that something has been lost to freedom as well as to the market when it refuses to condemn protest which is vicious. But it is something worse if it turns out that Parliament is prepared to pander to populism and to protest. It has a longer and better tradition of trying to see where the balance of right and wrong lies, where the evidence points, and how to assess the competing claims of interest groups. Having done so, it has usually recognised that emerging principles and ideals need to be applied fairly.

If new sensitivities emerge, and new principles are promulgated, people have a right to see them applied consistently: that is what it means to have equality before the law. That is, if a ban is good for the goose, it is good for the gander too. On such elementary principles we can see that only ill-considered idealism would stigmatise, let alone outlaw, the fur trade and its customers. Public morality is offended by such a ban, with or without compensation for its victims.

# Appendix 1

Extracts from a conversation with one of Denmark's most senior mink husbandry academic researchers, Professor Lief Lau Jeppesen, of the Zoological Institute, University of Copenhagen.

## On the comparison of mink and other farmed animals

Compared with other farm animals we have these mink in the wild, and that makes a difference. Researchers can study mink and foxes in the wild, so it is easier to consider them. They really are not the same as their domestic equivalents. We know that domestication takes place very fast at the beginning. There are changes in behaviour, primarily, and that is very fast because those that do not reproduce are heavily selected against from the very the beginning.

But we have scientific argument which shows that the brains of farmed mink are smaller than those of wild mink. That is the case in all farm animal species and in mink it is reduced to almost the same extent as the other domesticated species compared with their wild cousins... they are calmer and they are less easy to stress. Maybe they are also more stupid.

There's a difference and we see it in all domestic species, in cats and dogs for instance. I do not know the reason or function of the difference in brain size, but I think it favours the species. I simply want to use it favour of saying there a certain degree of domestication.

It is cruelty to keep wild mink under the same conditions as farmed mink and it is simply not allowed.

I think it is very important to compare mink with other domesticated species, for instance, dogs, cats and cattle. They are all able to survive in the wild given the right conditions. Domesticated pigs have been released to pig parks for study reasons and they survive very well - the pigs need the right food and they are restricted when they are set free because in most places you have to feed them for a while, but if there are not too many of them they can survive quite well in woods. Battery hens can live in the wild. The same holds for cattle: when you release them for grazing, they take care of themselves all summer. And they are indeed rather wild and difficult to handle when you capture them in the autumn.

I agree that the conditions for farmed mink are better than the conditions for intensively kept pigs and chicken, though you cannot in a scientific way compare the two. I have seen them both.

It is not hard to see the difference. You can compare the way you keep mink. It allows one individual to survive and reproduce in the same sort of environment for life. They live for several years and for much longer than they are able to survive in the wild. That is not true of the pig. The breeding pig is kept in better conditions than the pig kept only for food. But all mink are kept in the same environment, one which allows breeding. They are allowed the same standard whether for breeding or fur production.

### On weaning

Weaning is at 7-8 weeks usually, but it is very important to understand the way they are weaned then. The mother is removed and it is a good time to remove her because if it was delayed she would be very exhausted. Then all her pups are kept all together for another 2-3 weeks, and then kept in pairs. It is very bad for the animals to keep them singly from an early age, and that is true for most species of developed mammals.

The production mink, at 10 or 11 weeks old (in the summer). has got another 3-4 months to live (until slaughter in the late autumn).. It needs warmth and comfort early on. In the wild it wants food and in the spring time it wants to mate. If we compare pigs, fattening pigs are removed at 4 weeks of age, which is much earlier than in the wild and relatively and relatively it is much earlier than happens to mink in farms.

In wild mink the young start feeding solid food at 5-6-8 weeks and that is when mother brings solid food to the den, so it is gradual. At 10-11 weeks you see kits alone outside the nest without their mothers and so it seems that the weaning process on farms is nearer to the wild situation as compared with sows or pigs. If we compare breeding pigs, the sow is mated again one week after the weaning and so it is much harder working compared to the wild. In the wild, sows might have two litters a years but on a farm they are often forced to deliver many times a year.

It is very difficult to know about specific needs in farm animals. They need food, shelter and to mate. In the wild, the mink is a solitary species. When they are solitary in the wild they need big territories to find food and for that reason maybe they are not that hostile when they have plenty of food. We are experimenting with group housing, to see what is the ideal number of animals per group for a given cage size.

My experiments show that they benefit from being together, but not for all of the Autumn, for instance. It seems to be an advantage that the litter is kept all together in right amount of space up until August or September but after that they are more aggressive towards each other. So after that, they should be in pairs, and we are examining putting them in pairs then. But not if they are they are adult and unknown to each other.

When it comes to group management, an average litter has five young. We tried to keep them and their mother, six animals, together in three normal cages, which is the same stocking density as keeping them in pairs. The advantage is that each animal has more freedom of movement, and it seems as if they develop less stereotypies as adults. But during the Autumn you cannot see the difference.

You see stereotypies in the animals that go on to breed. Stereotypy is an adult characteristic in mink at least. You hardly see it in the production animals. It is seen for the first time in November and it is significant only in January or February, and then when they are preoccupied with breeding (in the Spring). it falls again.

A domestic cat gets restless before it is fed, and I agree that this could be an explanation for a lot of stereotypy, that it is just excitement which has to be expressed in a relatively little area. I think that the physical limitation on the behaviour looks like stereotypy, and it is hard to see whether it is actually psychotic.

It is very difficult to say that an unhappy mink will show stereotypy. I think there's too much emphasis on stereotypy as a measure. In all other respects they thrive, reproduce and the level of basic stress hormones is quite normal and they are not afraid of humans, at least not to an extent to stress them. But they have this smaller question of performing stereotypy behaviour or behaviour which looks like stereotypy.

It is possible to reduce the occurrence of stereotypy, mainly by feeding more frequently in January and February. There are two reasons. One is that at that time animals have less to do and they are alone. And the other reason is that they get slightly less feed than they would prefer and that has to do with farmers wanting to feed them as much as possible around pelting. But later on when they are used as breeding animals they should be less fat and so they get less food than they want. So you can reduce it by letting them feeding them more frequently.

## On measuring distress and stress

We are not near knowing whether a creature is happy or unhappy just by measuring hormone. The answer to any welfare question is to look at many measures.

We know for sure that when animals are acutely stressed - scared - there is an increase in stress hormones so it is very easy to measure acute stress. But then you have to consider the circumstance, the context of the rise in stress hormones, because they rise when you perform mating behaviour or eat or badly stressed, because they prepare the body for violent action, so the acute hormone is not much use in the welfare discussion.

But the signs of welfare problems are long term stress, which shows as raised cortisone and cortisol levels, which are a pair of the hormones involved. If the base levels of these are permanently raised they are indicative of a difficult situation. The base level is the level in the blood stream, it is the mean level, but for stress hormones its not quite fair to talk about base levels. These hormones are excreted in episodes every half hour or hour and it is not regular. But it maintains a certain level in the blood which is the base level, and then, when you are stressed, there is a three or four fold increase, but the base level may be raised by 50 per cent, as measured as an average across time.

I think you can say that the cortisol levels are indicative of poor condition. It is raised in all situations where we expect animals not to fare well and it has causal consequences for all the life process. It begins in a bad effect and it produces a bad effect. Stressed animals are prepared for violent action all the time, they draw on their reserves of food and fat and the blood is filled with free fatty acids and blood sugar and they break down food stuffs and reserves all the time and they spend a lot more energy in being in the situation of preparedness. Blood is moved to muscles and brain and away from digestion and that is why they lose weight in this situation.

But animals can show stereotypy without showing these stress signs. If it is real psychotic behaviour, it is a means of coping and a means of doing something that regulates the stress hormones downwards. So animals showing stereotypy often show the lowest base levels of stress hormones and that is why you cannot evaluate these measure out of context.

If there are problems in animals, they have problems with breeding optimally, and that is in part due to the causal relationship between stress hormones and reproductive hormones. The reproductive hormones are reduced when there's a lot of stress hormone. There's an active inhibition and that may be evolutionarily adaptive, because there's no point starting breeding in very stressful environments.

### On needs, for instance, swimming and occupation

Mink certainly need food and drinking water, and mating, they also maybe need activity because they are adapted to being swift, active, opportunistic hunters. So it is fair to imagine that they are adapted to being adaptive and to having something to manage in elements of their lives, and that could be a specific need which we have to fulfil and which is not fulfilled for the time being, these animals certainly have a need for a den, for somewhere to hide, and you can easily show that if you close the next box then they develop all the signs of long term stress and really demonstrate bad welfare. But I do not think swimming is a need in this species and that is because they do not need to swim to maintain their life functions.

Chicken or hens, they have a need for dust-bathing, and we know that for sure and it is quite natural. They have to do that dust-bathing to keep their feathers in good condition in the wild and the most easy way for natural selection to take care of that is to put into the animals an internal need for that behaviour. But chickens can keep the feathers in good condition without dust-bathing, but there remains a need to perform the motions of dust-bathing and you can compare it with the need for food.

In the wild mink, live close to water and at some Times of the year they get most of their food from water. But in periods in which there are plenty of voles or young rabbits, they can feed on the terrestrial animals and then they never go to the water. So they have no daily need to go to water for instance.

Then we have the Oxford work which has shown that mink will lift heavy burdens to get to water and here I think we are dealing not with a specific need but a need to be active and to do something and that means it is not necessary for us to provide water but to provide some sort of occupation.

We might make mink work for food. They do learn easily, and that is a possible way to make their lives more interesting - but it is not without limit. In the wild, they take large meals and long periods in the den.

We know having a lot of straw is good occupation: they make new nests.

We are talking about need and occupation, and the best environmental enrichment is another mink. That is the best dynamic enrichment and they thrive very well in pairs. But whether housing in bigger groups helps the animals or the politicians, I'm not so sure.

The difficulty with making feeding more interesting is that it probably needs dry feed, and wet feed is much better for the mink. Similarly, providing water is difficult because it brings disease problems as well as expense.

## On carbon dioxide

I think the Oxford work on carbon dioxide is right: mink can smell it and they dislike it, but they have to be killed anyway and it is very difficult to imagine an affordable method which is better than carbon dioxide. They are killed fast and with no pain and there's a difference between pain and dislike. They realise that something is wrong but do not know what is wrong, and it is not actually hurting them. Carbon monoxide really kills you without notice, you cannot smell it. But we do not use it with mink because you do not want that huge amount of carbon monoxide around: it is too good a killer.

# Appendix 2

A note and extracts of a conversation with an international negotiator on humane trapping standards.

Neal Jotham is a lifelong animal welfare worker. Volunteer with Canadian Association for Humane Trapping, 14 years; Executive Director, Canadian Federation of Humane Societies, 8 years; former co-ordinator, Humane Trapping Program, Department of Environment, 14 years; member of the Canadian delegation to the negotiations of the Agreement on International Humane Trapping Standards, chairman of the ISO, the International Organisation for Standardisation's Technical Committee on Animal (Mammal) Traps.

## A Note On the Agreement Upon International Humane Trapping Standards

### By Neal Jotham

Commencing in 1987, starting with 7 countries, through to 1994, with 15 countries, an ISO Technical Committee (191) worked to develop international humane trapping standards that would have included allowable trap performance thresholds. This work happened to coincide with one of the conditions set out in a 1994 EU regulation that prohibits importation of products derived from 12 North American wild fur-bearers unless:

1) an exporting country prohibited the use of the leghold trap

OR

2) the trapping methods used for the species listed in the regulation meet internationally agreed humane trapping standards.

The ISO TC 191 process was underway long before the EU fur ban regulation was being contemplated and several European animal protection organisations were invited to join those deliberations, but initially refused the invitation. When, in 1992,

EU officials were contemplating the drafting of the regulation, they recognised that a fur ban regulation could very well contravene the rules of the WTO. They were also informed that simply banning a particular trapping device would not improve animal welfare (a supposed intention of the regulation) if indeed trapping would continue and use any methods at all so long as they did not include leghold traps.

The answer was to take into account the ISO trap standards-setting process and since the 1994 regulation was to come into effect in 1996, thereby giving time for the ISO standards to be completed, the officials included condition 2 in the regulation.

Animal protection organisations who were vehemently opposed to the fur trade, regardless of how humane it is, contemplated, what for them was a loophole in the regulation (the aspect of humane trapping standards) and considered that it could potentially allow the wild fur trade to continue in Europe. Consequently, in 1994 they embraced the ISO process and did everything possible to undermine the work that had been completed even though a major stated objective for any ISO standard setting process is 'to facilitate trade'

These groups demanded that the term 'humane' be removed from the ISO trap standards on grounds that the start-up, trap performance thresholds were unacceptable to be used in the context of their meaning of the term - requiring killing traps to effect instant death and restraining traps to cause no injury.

The difficulty was not in removing the term 'humane' from the ISO Standards, (improved animal welfare related to trapping was still being addressed through the performance thresholds), but rather in removing it in the context of its use in addressing condition 2 of the EU fur ban regulation. An EU Commission official made the situation more contentious by informing the ISO TC 191 meeting that 'if the term 'humane' is removed from the international standard, the standard could not be used as a condition for allowing the importation of wild fur products into EU countries'.

Ultimately, by 1996 consensus could not be reached for an ISO trap standard that contained performance thresholds and the work turned toward the development of ISO Standards for 'Trap Testing Methodologies'. This effort has culminated in the successful publication of those Standards in August 1999. This is not a minor conclusion to what became long and volatile deliberations. A major difficulty experienced, throughout the ISO TC 191 work, was the lack of comparable trap research and testing data. These new ISO Standards, when applied by any country for determining trap performance, are designed eliminate that controversy. This is extremely important in the context of the Agreement on International Humane Trapping Standards.

In 1995, in the absence of ISO Standards that included the term 'humane' and trap performance thresholds as well as consideration of the fact that a challenge under the WTO rules would not be constructive and should be avoided if at all possible, Canada, the EU, Russia and the USA decided to attempt to negotiate, on a government to government basis, the development of international humane trapping standards. This effort was successful with the signing of the Agreement on International Humane Trapping Standards in December 1997, by Canada, the EU and Russia and a slightly different one between EU and the United States.

### Neal Jotham: remarks from a conversation...

Now we have to test the traps according to a standard, which is what we were working for before - we have now negotiated politically an agreement which is a standard to replace the ISO standard in which we've got performance requirements. The animal rights people do not like those performance requirements. They've tried desperately to stop this Agreement - but there it is, there it sits.

We have to deliver, absolutely, and we've got various time frames, between five and eight years to do the job and bring in legislation and to ban traps that do not meet the standards. And we're doing marvellously, I'm very pleased to say. Canada is really moving along. We're co-operating with the United States -

because trapping is carried out closer to more urban areas they need to use more restraining systems that they will have to test than what we do. They're willing to accept the sort of things that we're doing with killing traps and we're working with them on restraining traps.

We believe that leghold traps of some kind for some species will meet the standards. We have said we want to be able to retain some sort of legholding traps for wolf, coyote, lynx, bobcat and for racoon in some trapping conditions in Canada. In the United States there's more species. I would add only red fox, bear and perhaps arctic fox in Canada although they're not on the list at the moment.

The negotiations about 'humane' trapping standards were made difficult because even a humane killing trap does not deliver an instant kill all the time. Depending on the species, it can have levels of killing performance in the range of 180 or 200 seconds for some species in some circumstances. But the animal rights people said absolutely no, the only way you can use the word humane, was if it delivered an instant kill; or if it is a holding type trap, there should be no injury. That is a total impossibility and it cannot be done here in Europe and it is not done here in Europe. So you're looking at gradual, realistic change within an industry where you are working out in the wilderness, in the bush, in rivers and under the ice, etc. where you do not the conditions you have in a slaughterhouse where you have virtually total control or in a laboratory where you have got laboratory rats under your control. So now, you have to be realistic and say OK, what can do we do in such a situation when trapping will continue for many reasons?

Canada, the United States and Russia and others asked the EU Commission what are you doing about trapping in Europe, how do your traps perform? You have banned the leghold trap for whatever your reasons, saying it is terrible. Fine, so have we, for a number of species. But five or six blocks from the European parliament in Brussels we walked down to a hardware store and asked the clerk, do you have anything that can be used to catch foxes? Do you have traps?' The clerk brought out a leghold trap with teeth in it, and sold it to us (Such a trap is wholly illegal in Canada - RDN).

What we're asked to do by the Agreement is to achieve a killing time of between 45 seconds for ermine, 120 seconds for marten and for the larger animals such as racoon and beaver up to 300 seconds with the caveat of trying to lower those as best we can over the years with research and testing. That is what is set out in the Agreement on International Humane Trapping Standards. We've directed our whole trap research and testing programme towards addressing the circumstances in that agreement.

## On the leghold trap or any type of restraining device

The Agreement requires that the conventional steel-jawed leghold restraining trap be prohibited in Canada by April 2001 for 5 of the listed species. It has already been prohibited for 7 of the listed species. However, as I said previously there will likely be some type of legholding traps for several species that will meet the standards.

The holding of a wild animal in any type of restraining device is likely going to cause it some difficulty and stress simply because it is being held in a place it does not want to be. Most of the wild predator animals that are trapped have a tremendous ability for adapting to a stressful event as a built-in survival mechanism and when traps are set by the professional trapper in a way that allows them to get under cover, struggling against the trap is minimised and therefore injuries are minimised.

The point is that all restraining traps used for whatever reason to capture the species listed in the Agreement will have to comply with the Standards set out in it and those that do not meet the Standards prohibited by 2007. For restraining traps they will have to demonstrate that none of a list of specific injuries occurs in 80% of a sample of 20 animals caught in such traps. Believe me the Standard is tough.

Yes, the leghold trap with teeth was banned years ago in Canada and the USA and yet in Brussels we could buy what is referred to as the old English gin trap. The old leghold trap with teeth hardly needed to be banned in Canada because it simply just fell out of use. Why? Because they cut the animal up and it struggled excessively usually causing damage to its pelt. Furthermore if an animal broke some bones allowing it to twist out of the trap it is gone, so that is not very economical for a trapper. Any rate the whole issue of leghold traps was obviously more a political move than a true concern for animal welfare The animal rights/anti-fur people thought, if they could force a ban on the leghold trap then there would be a dent in the trade. If Canada had simply just taken a political step and said we're banning all leghold traps it would not have stopped trapping. But the systems and devices used may have been more cruel or more inhumane.

Implementation of the Agreement ensures that traps will meet a Standard that improves the welfare of animals regardless of the reason they are trapped.

### On the killing trap (submersion systems)

In Canada beaver and muskrat, otter, mink, are semi-aquatic species which can be taken in an underwater circumstance where they will be killed either by a killing trap itself or very quickly through carbon dioxide narcosis in a holding trap. People identify this with a human drowning, but actually it is asphyxiation. The reason is this: a semi-aquatic species such as beaver caught in a trap properly set will automatically dive under water because it has been frightened. It can survive under water for 15-odd minutes so it is not starting to die the moment it goes under water. That is the same for a human only humans cannot stay under so long. In the case of the beaver, its heart slows down, it never opens its oesophagus, it has the ability to shunt blood from the outer tissues of its body to the brain for a period of time. Automatically the heart slows down as soon as it dives, so it has the ability to live underwater, until if it is under there long enough an internal exchange takes place of carbon dioxide for the oxygen. The blood finally runs out of oxygen and none gets to the brain and carbon dioxide replaces the oxygen and so it dies. It is a death not unlike what happens when people kill animals in animal rescue shelters using a gas method, or when carbon dioxide is used in killing laboratory rats for example.

## On the killing trap used on land

The effect of banning steel-jawed leghold traps on land was not a great hardship because the trappers themselves had been changing without any push from anywhere and other traps were coming available. A new killing type trap came forward in the early 60s It is called the Conibear trap . The reason it is so good is that it can replace the leghold trap as one of the most efficient devices for capturing a large number of species in a variety of trapping situations. That had been one of the major obstacles to making change - how do you get devices that are as efficient for the trapper as the leghold and can be set in so many various places? So, once that became resolved things started to change and it was quite remarkable.

Killing traps will work on land, for capturing beaver muskrat, the martens, fisher, racoon, squirrels, all the sort of terrestrial species up to a certain size, racoon and beaver size being probably a good break off. With coyote, first of all you have to think it is about twice or maybe three bigger than a fox - just imagine the size of trap that you might have to have.

## On welfare backfire

Of course, in trapping you want to kill every animal instantly, but let me give you an example of the kind of foolish thinking that goes on sometimes. In Massachusetts in the US, the animal rights people were successful to have the State virtually ban the use of traps for even control purposes. Never mind just for trade, for fur: you cannot use traps to take animals unless you can prove absolutely there is a need to have this animal killed or whatever. Well, now they're suddenly experiencing problems with the population growth of beaver and rural people and people that have cottages and so forth are starting to complain to the government. They are saying, "My God, the beavers are down the rivers and they've built dams and they're flooding my property I've got to get rid of them. Who can I turn to?" And the government wildlife people, say, "Sorry, but there's no way we can do anything unless you can prove absolutely the damage is being done and if so all you can do is go out there and capture them with live traps of some sort." You will then take them and you can shoot them or give them an overdose of barbiturate or something.

So let is explore the animal welfare aspect of this. The trapper could go out, take the animal, kill it within 180 seconds, probably less. Instead, people have to capture this thing which means it is going to be held in the range of 4-6 hours, because it will likely be caught at night, and the guy comes around in the morning and then they've got to take it some place, unless they have a veterinarian with them, and have it shot or injected. Now where's the welfare aspect in that? It almost borders on what the philosopher George Santyana defines as fanaticism. That is, it is 'redoubling your effort when you've forgotten your aim'.

Of course, they meant well. Fine. But wait a minute, just because you hate trapping, or you hate the fur trade so much and if that is your aim, to stop somehow the fur trade, then what does it matter about animal welfare - it does not mean anything.

## On the need for trapping

There are something in the range of 80,000 trappers operating in Canada in a given year - a great many of whom are native people. In a lot of cases they have no other opportunities and it provides a very substantial part of their annual income. What does this mean? If you look at the price of the pelts, and the number they took, they got $400-500 dollars a year. So people might say, that is chicken feed - tell them to do something else, train them on something else. Well that is typically not going to happen in those kinds of communities in the North.

When we have a lowering in prices, some of the more southerly trappers will say 'I'm not going to go out and trap - I was actually using trapping to supplement my income because I needed to, I work in the local mill, but I'm not going this year because the price of the pelt of a beaver is $7 instead of $20 - it cost me $5 to get the thing in the first place with my equipment' and so on and so forth. So he does not go. But the interesting thing is in some of the more northerly native communities the numbers of trappers will almost remain constant because they have to go - they need the two dollars, and that also applies for many non-natives as well.

# Appendix 3

Conversations with North American trappers and official conservationists.

## 1) Sandy, 76, trapper and veteran, from Cross Lake, Manitoba, Canada

When we heard that our country was at war, we wanted to fight for the mother country, for England and for freedom. So I joined up, and we trained 6 months here in Canada and then for two years in England. We were in the front line at Normandy and then during the rest of the war, in Germany. We wanted to fight for freedom and for the freedom to use the animals and land which God had given us to use. It is not right to neglect the animals which God has put there for our use.

## 2) Alan McCloud, trapper, Cross Lake, Manitoba, Canada

People who trap find they can be proud to be an Indian. When you're out on the land it gives you an awareness of the land and your responsibilities. You cannot afford to make a mistake. No, you cannot really make a living at it. You can offset some of the expenses, put money towards a skidoo, toward the high prices at the store, etc. We have power dams here which are a hundred times more damaging than trapping and cause much more suffering when they flood the animals' homes. My mum and Dad did not give up trapping until they died and when I was young there were eight of us kids and we all went trapping, there was not anything else. Between eight and 16 that was all we did. I go trapping now because it is in my blood. A very small minority of the young will go out trapping now compared with 20 years ago. I'm 57 (in 1996) and nowadays there's better education and more opportunity for working at different things.

## On welfare

There should be more purpose to it, they should work for welfare which they're able to do. I defend trapping because you're doing something, by learning that you have responsibility for yourself and for your self-esteem.

A small minority of mink suffer, if they're trapped in warm weather, on land. Near water, they're caught in a leghold trap and the animal drowns in the water and does not suffer. In cold weather, in open country, they die of cold.

### 3) Bob Carmichael, conservation official with Manitoba State, Canada, working on fur issues from 1973

Without any doubt it was a sense of wonder which propelled me to the area. It was seeing flights of duck in October against an autumn moon and seeing otter playing in the creek.

I feel very good about trapping. When you look at the wider picture of what trapping achieves. Trapping is not eternally right or eternally wrong. It saves provincial treasuries millions of dollars a year from animal damage (And granted the natural risk of accident and the probability of a nasty death in nature). I know if trapping stopped we would be increasing the net amount of suffering to animals. I believe very strongly that the net effect of buying a fur coat is to decrease animal suffering and to contribute to human well-being.

I have seen animals trapped wrongly and they suffer horribly.

It just bothers me intensely when just a small minority of people, people with big egos and fat wallets, succeed in selling a whole notion which simply is not true. The animal rights people have very successfully made the Government the Goliath to their David and they are much cleverer than us in dealing with the media and wrapping a red ribbon round their package.

## 4) Noel Kinlear, conservation official with the State of Louisiana, USA

[Farmed] nutria escaped from a pen during a hurricane, and because they were thought to be helpful against the invasion of water hyacinth people caught them and took them to their own parts and by 1953 they were everywhere. Perhaps there were 20 million in Louisiana, and damaging sugar cane and rice production quite severely. By 1955 the problem was severe enough to warrant their being listed as 'Outlaw' species and a 25 cent bounty was placed on their heads, but this was never paid because funds were never made available. There was market in the early 60s: pelt prices created demand and more nutria were harvested than muskrat for the first time. But then there was a fashion shift from long hair fur to short hair, especially in the main market, Germany, and by mid to late 80s it fell continuously until in 1985 only about 150,000-250,000 were taken annually. Below a cull of about 500,000 they begin to notice more damage.

Louisiana has 40 per cent of the US coastal wetland and they are depended upon for hundreds of species, including wading birds, gulls, terns, and then in the water there's oyster, blue crab, vital economic fisheries, alligators. And northern water fowl winter here, so there's damage to these species we love to see and need to see.

In the open country you can shoot, but the majority of the acreage here is swamplands, or where there's rank vegetation, so you cannot ride through them and see nutria to shoot them.

Our strategy as the agency which manages wildlife is to try to get the economic value of nutria pelt and the meat up so that we do not have to force the taxpayer to cover the cull with their money.

# References

Brown, Antony (1974): *Who Cares for Animals: 150 years of the RSPCA*, London: Heinemann.

Budiansky, Stephen (1994) *The Covenant of the Wild: Why animals chose domestication*, London: Weidenfeld & Nicolson.

Cooper, J, Mason, G and Raj, M (1998): 'Determination of the aversion of farmed mink (*mustela vison*) to carbon dioxide,' *The Veterinary Record*, September 26.

CUAWIC (No date): Cambridge University Animal Welfare Information Centre, *Report on the welfare of farmed mink and foxes in relation to housing and management*, by Dr A J Nimon, and D. M Broom. Cambridge University: Dept of Clinical Veterinary Medicine.

*Daily Telegraph* (1997): Obituary, October 3.

*Daily Telegraph* (1998a): Johnny Beardsall, 'He ain't nasty - but he is a killer,' September 5.

*Daily Telegraph* (1998b): Peter Birkett, 'Vet under siege,' August 1.

*Daily Telegraph* (1999e): Hilary Alexander, 'Animal Passions,' July 19.

*Daily Telegraph* (1999a): Louise Jury, 'ICA picks hunting Tory as chairman,' May 23.

*Daily Telegraph* (1999c): Charles Clover, 'Europe kicks up a stink over British move to ban mink,' May 13.

*Daily Telegraph* (1999d): 'Animal rights group shackle farmer's wife,' 10 June.

Dawkins, Marian (1993): *Through Our Eyes Only?: The search for animal consciousness*, Oxford: Freeman.

Diamond, Jared (1997): *Why Is Sex Fun?* London: Weidenfeld & Nicolson.

Eagle, Maria (1999): 'I am very pleased my Bill will bring to an end what is a barbaric practice to produce an inessential luxury item. My Bill has the backing of 74 per cent of the British public who support a ban on fur farming,' Press release, 23 February.

*The Economist* (1999): 'Jungle stuff,' August 7.

*Evening Standard* (1999): C. Croft, 'Gilding the lily in the class of '99,' 8 June.

*The Express* (1999): Tracy McVeigh, 'Naomi on the catwalk, looking sheepish in wolf's clothing,' February 18.

FAWC (1989): Farm Animal Welfare Council, Press Release, April 4.

Guardian (1997): Susannah Frankel, 'Fur's big comeback snares supermodel: objections to pelts may be just skin deep,' March 8.

Hansen, Steffen (1995): 'Production conditions, behaviour and welfare of farmed mink,' Foulum, Denmark: The National Institute of Animal Science, Department of Research in Small Animals, April.

Harri, Mikko, Nurminen, Lijsa, Filen, Tuula (1995): 'Stomach ulcer as an indicator of stress in farm mink,' *Acta Agric. Scand. Seci. Animal Sci.*, 45, 204-207.

Hill, Christopher (1975): *The World Turned Upside Down*, London: Penguin.

*The Independent* (1999) A. Jankiewic, 'Cattery closure delights protesters,' August 14.

Johnson, Paul (1991): *The Birth of the modern: World society, 1815-1830*, London: Weidenfeld and Nicolson.

Kelsall, Len (1999): Telephone conversations and a meeting with chairman of the British Fur Breeders' Association, February.

Lawson-Cruttenden, T. and Addison, N. (1997): *Blackstone's Guide to the Protection From Harassment Act*, London: Blackstone.

Leach, Gerald (1976) *Energy and Food Production*, London: IPC Science and Technology.

Mason, G. (1999): 'Improving the welfare of farmed mink: Do physiological responses to deprivation mirror behavioural measures of the importance of environment enrichment?' Note for the Universities Federation for Animal Welfare.

Miller, Geoffrey (1999): 'In Defence of Waste: Evolution and consumerism,' *Prospect,* February.

*New Scientist* (1999): P. Aldhous, Andy Coghlan, and Jon Copley, 'Animal experiments: where do you draw the line? Let the people speak,' 22 May.

North, Richard D (forthcoming): *Risk: the Human Adventure,* Cambridge: European Science and Environment Forum.

Rouvinen, Kirsti (1999): Telephone conversation.

Sapolsky, Robert (1994): *Why Zebras Do not Get Ulcers,* New York: Freeman.

Scruton, Roger (1996): *Animal Rights and Wrongs,* London: Demos.

Skovgaard, K., Jeppesen, L. L. and Hansen, C. P. B. (1997): 'Would you like a swim, madam mink?' *Scientifur* 21 (7): 247-251.

Spruijt, B. M. (1996): 'The Plan of Approach for the benefit of improving the welfare of mink examined further', Yalelaan, Holland: Interfaculty Animal Welfare Centre.

*Sunday Telegraph* (1998a): J. Knowsley, 'I'm scared, says dying hunger striker,' December 6.

*Sunday Telegraph* (1998b): Time Reid, 'Why I quit the evil animal fanatics,' August 16.

*Sunday Telegraph* (1998c): Colin Blakemore, 'I will talk to those who threaten to murder me,' December 6.

*Sunday Telegraph* (1999): L. Mills and C. Milner, 'Saatchi puts shock-art on menu of planned Sensation restaurant,' July 18.

*Sunday Times* (1998a): Profile, 'Barry Horne: An animal passion with murder in its heart,' December 6 1998

Thomas, Keith (1984): *Man and the Natural World,* London: Penguin.

*The Times* (1997): Obituary, October 11.

*The Times* (1998a) Simon Jenkins, 'Of mink and men', August 12.

*The Times* (1998b): Lucy Pinney, 'What is so awful about mink?' August 15.

*The Times* (1998c): Law Report, European Court of Human Rights, 'Breach of human rights in arrest for peaceful protest,' October 1.

*The Times* (1999a): Joanna Bale, 'A nice, clean place to die,' March 6.

*The Times* (1999b): Joanna Bale, 'MPs support Bill to close mink farms in three years', March 6.

*The Times* (1999c) M. Binyon, 'New style terrorist is a lone fanatic,' May 4.

*The Times* (1999d) Law Report, House of Lords, 'Demonstration not trespassory assembly,' March 5.

*The Times* (1999e): Andrew Pierce, 'City riot wins favour with the 'eco-kids': £2m damage seen as part of fight for 'new world order'.

*The Times* (1999f) Lucy Pinney, 'Intensive, yes, but not cruel', December 2.

Webster, John (1994): *Animal Welfare: A cool eye towards Eden*, Oxford: Blackwells Science.

Widdecombe, Anne (1998) Television debate: Nothing But the Truth, Channel Four, March 7.

Wiepkema, P. R. (1994) *Advice on husbandry on fur animals in the Netherlands: Recommendations on Mink Farming*, translation of advice to Dutch Agric. Ministry, available from author.